As You Like It

EDITED BY
George Lyman Kittredge

Revised by Irving Ribner

William Shakespeare

As You Like It

JOHN WILEY & SONS, INC.

New York   London   Sydney   Toronto

ISBN 0 471 00509 6

LIBRARY OF CONGRESS CATALOG CARD NUMBER: 66-30745

PRINTED IN THE UNITED STATES OF AMERICA.

10 9 8 7 6 5 4

PREFACE

The New Kittredge Shakespeares

The publication of George Lyman Kittredge's *Complete Works of Shakespeare* in 1936 was a landmark in Shakespeare scholarship. The teacher who for almost half a century had dominated and shaped the direction of Shakespearean study in America produced what was recognized widely as the finest edition of Shakespeare up to his time. In the preface to this edition Kittredge indicated his editorial principles; these allowed a paramount authority to the Folio of 1623 and countenanced few departures from it while, at the same time, refusing to "canonize the heedless type-setters of the Elizabethan printing house." Kittredge's work was marked by a judicious conservatism and a common sense rarely found in equal measure in earlier editors of Shakespeare. In the thirty-odd years which have gone by since the appearance of this monumental volume, however, considerable advances have been made in the establishment of Shakespeare's text, and our body of knowledge about the dates, sources, and general historical background of Shakespeare's plays has vastly increased. The present revision is designed to apply this new knowledge to Kittredge's work so that it may have as much value to the student and general reader of today as it had to those of thirty years ago.

Before his death Kittredge had issued, in addition to *The Complete Works*, separate editions of sixteen of the plays, each copiously annotated. Some of the notes were unusually elaborate, but they interpreted Shakespeare's language with a fullness and precision attained by few other commentators, for Kittredge had few equals in his intimate knowledge of Elizabethan English. In freshly annotating the plays I have, accordingly, tried to use

Kittredge's own notes as fully as space would permit. Where I have repeated his distinctive language or recorded his characteristic critical opinions, I have followed the note with the symbol [κ]; where Kittredge's definition of a term can be found in essentially the same words in other editions, I have not used the identifying symbol. Every annotator draws upon the full body of the notes of earlier editors, and to give credit for every note is impossible. Notes have been placed at page bottoms.

The brief introductions which Kittredge wrote for the plays have been replaced by new ones, for what seemed like indisputable fact some thirty years ago often appears today to be much more uncertain, and many new issues of which Kittredge was not aware have been raised in recent criticism. The new introductions seek to present what are now generally agreed to be basic facts about the plays and to give some indications of the directions which modern criticism has taken, although specific analyses of individual plays are avoided.

Such great authority attaches to Kittredge's text that it has not frequently — and never lightly — been departed from. Where changes have been made, they have usually involved the restoration of copy-text readings now generally accepted in place of the emendations of eighteenth- and nineteenth-century editors of which Kittredge, in spite of his extraordinary conservatism in this regard, sometimes too easily approved. Only rarely has an emendation been adopted in the present revision which was not also adopted by Kittredge. All departures from the copy-texts are indicated in the notes, emendations followed by the names of the editors by whom they were first proposed. Wherever Kittredge's text has been departed from for any reason, his reading is given in the notes. Modern spelling has in a few instances been substituted for Elizabethan forms which are mere spelling variations but which Kittredge nevertheless retained. His punctuation has not been altered except in a few very rare instances.

The system of recording elisions and contractions which Kittredge explained in his introduction to *The Complete Works* has been retained, as has his method of preserving to the fullest the copy-text stage directions, with all additions to them enclosed within square brackets. Although modern editors recognize the vagueness of the place settings of Elizabethan plays and are reluctant to include the place designations so favoured by eighteenth- and nineteenth-century editors, much historical interest nevertheless attaches to these, and Kittredge's place designations accordingly have been retained between square brackets. Kittredge's attempt to retain the line numbering of the Globe text, which resulted in considerable irregularity in prose passages, has been abandoned, and the lines of each play have been freshly numbered. Kittredge's act and scene divisions have been retained, as has his practice of surrounding by square brackets those divisions which are not in the copy-texts.

The *New Kittredge Shakespeares* include individual editions of each of the plays, the sonnets, and the minor poems, and a new edition of *The Complete Works* in a single volume. A comprehensive introduction to Shakespeare's life, times, and theatrical milieu is available both as a separate volume and as an introduction to *The Complete Works.*

IRVING RIBNER

INTRODUCTION

As You Like It

⸻

◇◇◇◇◇
◇◇◇◇◇ That *As You Like It* was an extremely popular play in
◇◇◇◇◇ its own time we may infer from an entry in the Stationers' Register for August 4, 1600, which directed that this play,
along with three others belonging to the Lord Chamberlain's
Men "be stayed" — that is, be reserved for printing by a particular publisher, although not printed immediately. That this "stay-
ing entry" was a device by Shakespeare's company to prevent the
piracy of one of their most valuable properties we may be fairly
certain, and it apparently was successful, for *As You Like It* was
not printed before its inclusion in the First Folio (F¹) of 1623.
This is a good text, with relatively few errors and with full act
and scene divisions. It is followed closely in the present edition,
the few departures from it being indicated in the notes.

Since the play is not mentioned by Francis Meres in his *Pal-
ladis Tamia* of 1598, and since at III.v.80–1 Shakespeare alludes
clearly to Christopher Marlowe's poem *Hero and Leander,* which
was not published until 1598, the play usually has been dated
between 1598 and 1600. Jaques' speech "All the world's a stage"
(II.vii.138–65) seems to have specific reference to the name which
Shakespeare's company chose for the Globe Theatre when it was
built in 1599, and there is thus some reason to suppose that *As
You Like It* was among the first plays to be performed in that
structure. That it was written in late 1599 or early 1600 seems a
very reasonable supposition.

ROSALYNDE

As You Like It has rightfully been termed a "joyous" comedy,
for it is among the most lighthearted and carefree in tone and

spirit of all Shakespeare's plays. While the characters may seem at times to be beset with troubles and danger, we know always that these are merely the trials and tribulations of romantic story which must inevitably be reconciled before the tale is done. The forest in which the principal action occurs is neither the Arden of Shakespeare's native Warwickshire nor the Ardennes of Northern France which he found in his source, but a fantastic never-never-land full of strange animals and plants, a pastoral paradise deeply rooted in literary tradition, in which all of the problems of the world are resolved and where love is the only real concern of men and women who have escaped from care.

Much of the distinctive character of *As You Like It* we may trace to its source, for the play is a close dramatization of a prose romance which was itself one of the finest examples of the pastoral mode to appear in sixteenth-century England. Shakespeare's plot is taken directly from Thomas Lodge's *Rosalynde. Euphues golden legacie: found after his death in his Cell at Silexedra,* printed in 1590. In 1588 Lodge, a physician, poet, novelist, and writer of plays himself, had made a voyage to Terceras and the Canary Islands. In his dedication to Lord Hunsden he tells us that he wrote the novel to escape the tedium of the voyage, and in his address "To the Gentleman Readers," he says that he wrote it "in the Ocean, when euerie line was writ with a surge, and euerie humorous passion counterchekt with a storm," and he adds the sentence which apparently suggested to Shakespeare the title of his play: "If you like it, so." Shakespeare's use of Lodge's novel has been well described by Kittredge:

Shakespeare follows Lodge's story closely, but softens some of the more violent incidents. In Lodge, the quarrel with which the play begins is terrific. Saladyne (Shakespeare's Oliver) bids his servants lay hold on Rosader (Orlando) and bind him. Rosader "half mad" with wrath, though "of a mild and courteous nature," belabours them with a great rake and forces Saladyne to take refuge in a loft adjoining the garden. They make peace, Saladyne promising to reinstate Rosader in his proper rank in the family. After the wrestling match, in which the champion is killed, Rosader goes home with a troop of gentlemen. The door is shut against him, but he breaks it down, enters the hall, sword in hand, and feasts his companions royally. As soon as they are gone, Rosader draws his sword, resolved to be revenged on Saladyne, but peace is made once more, this time by the mediation of Adam Spencer. Shortly after, however, Saladyne surprises Rosader in his sleep and has him chained to a post. He is released by Adam, who tells him that Saladyne has informed their kindred and allies that he is insane and has invited them to breakfast next morning to see him chained up as a desperate madman. Adam fastens him once more to the post, but leaves the fetters unlocked. The guests are convinced that Rosader is mad indeed, and after dinner, heated with wine, they begin to rail at him. Adam gives a sign, Rosader breaks loose, and armed with poleaxes, they attack the guests, hurting many, killing some, and driving the rest out of the house. The sheriff of the county is summoned and vows to arrest Rosader. He and Adam break through the sheriff's posse and make their way to the Forest of Arden. There is no plot on Saladyne's part (as there is in Shakespeare) to murder his brother by burning down his lodging (II.III).

From this point the novel proceeds like the play. In the love story Shakespeare follows Lodge closely. Le Beau, Jaques, Touchstone, Audrey, William, and Sir Oliver Martext are Shakespeare's own. All the other important characters have their representatives in Lodge. The conclusion of the play is like that of the novel, except that Lodge's usurper, instead of being "converted both from his enterprise" against his brother (Shakespeare's Duke Senior) "and from the world" (V.IV.153–4), is killed in battle.

The novel is intensely Euphuistic in style and tells its tale in a leisurely fashion, but it has considerable merit. Like the play, it contains a number of love poems. The only character who is at all humorous is Coridon, and his humour is very mild indeed. The leisurely mode gives the novelist one advantage over the playwright: the conversion of the wicked brother seems less precipitate in Lodge than in Shakespeare; but this is at the expense of details which, in a play, would have retarded the action unduly at the close. Sudden conversion of the villain is often an imperative *coup de theatre* in comedy. . . . Perhaps Oliver is too lavishly rewarded for his penitence by the love of the charming Celia; but, after all, romance is not reality. "Every Jack must have his Jill" is a standard proverb for the dramatist.

Lodge's novel provides the three couples represented in Shakespeare by Orlando and Rosalind, Oliver and Celia, Silvius and Phebe; but in Lodge they are all denizens of a kind of romantic

fairyland that has slight contact with the actual. His Silvius and
Phebe, indeed, are purely pastoral figures of the conventional sort
— pleasant but quite artificial. In retaining the pastoral element
Shakespeare has set it off by contrast with the rivalry of Touchstone and William for the hand of Audrey — an episode of his own
felicitous invention; and thus he brings us into such intimate contact with the homely affairs of everyday life that we accept the
romance of fairyland without challenge.

THE TALE OF GAMELYN

For his own source Thomas Lodge had used a metrical romance
dating from the middle of the fourteenth century called *The
Tale of Gamelyn*. In Shakespeare's day it was wrongly believed
to have been by Chaucer, being identified with his missing
"Cook's Tale," and it has come down to us in manuscripts of
The Canterbury Tales. Since it was not printed until 1721, Lodge
must have had access to one such manuscript. That Shakespeare
himself may have consulted *Gamelyn* has been suggested but is
hardly likely.

What is important is that *Gamelyn* is one of a large body of
tales related to the story of Robin Hood. Gamelyn, or Will Gam-
well, is in fact the familiar Will Scarlet of the Robin Hood cycle.
The tale of a younger brother who escapes the oppression of a
wicked elder brother and with a faithful attendant escapes to the
woods and becomes the head of a band of outlaws, *Gamelyn,*
through Lodge's transformation of it, carries into Shakespeare's
play the romantic spirit of woodland adventure and good living
which we associate with Robin Hood and his band of "merry
men." In 1598 the Lord Admiral's Men, the chief rivals to Shakespeare's company, had produced a two-part play by Antony Mun-
day and Henry Chettle on the subject of Robin Hood: *The
Downfall of Robert Earl of Huntington after called Robin Hood*
and *The Death of Robert Earl of Huntington*. We have good
reason to believe that the *Huntington* plays were very popular,
and it has been suggested that *As You Like It* was written as a
counterattraction on the Robin Hood theme which might rival
their popularity.

THE PASTORAL WORLD

The pastoral tradition, which has its roots in the highly realistic *Idylls* of the Greek poet Theocritus, was developed in the *Eclogues* of Virgil, and in sixteenth-century Italy came to be widely expressed in drama and the novel as well as in poetry. Among the more influential of continental pastoral prose romances were the Italian *Arcadia* of Jacopo Sannazaro and the Spanish *Diana Inamorata* of Jorge de Montemayor. Both were widely known in Shakespeare's England, where they were drawn upon by Sir Philip Sidney in his *Arcadia*, the best known of Elizabethan pastoral novels and printed for the first time in the same year as Lodge's *Rosalynde*. It had, however, circulated in manuscript for some years and almost certainly was known to Lodge.

By Shakespeare's time the pastoral world had moved a long way from the Sicilian countryside of Theocritus; it had lost all relation to the world of reality. It was a magic land of escape where shepherds and shepherdesses tended their pure white sheep on hills of eternal summer, and where they had little to do but engage in fanciful intrigues and talk of love, defining it in the elegant rarified terms established by Italian Petrarchism. The shepherdesses of pastoral romance, with their fanciful names, were princesses in disguise, and the shepherds were philosophers as well as princes. Their talk tended to center about certain conventional themes: the nature of love, the relation of love to friendship, the pleasures of youth versus those of old age, and — perhaps most important of all — the joys of the country as opposed to the cares of city life, one way of expressing the ancient problem of the relation of nature to art and civilization, a theme which was to concern Shakespeare through much of his career, and which he was most perfectly to resolve in his final play, *The Tempest.*

Shakespeare intrudes into the artificial pastoral world he found in Lodge's romance the real world of rural England, most notably by means of his real rustics, Audrey and William, and by the satire of Touchstone who reduces the pastoral pretence to ridicule, just as he exposes the essential hollowness of the Petrarchan love conventions. In spite of this criticism of the pastoral ideal, Shakespeare nevertheless retains much of the flavour of the pastoral world. Silvius and Phebe are the typical lovers of pastoral romance, he the suffering swain and she the hardhearted mistress, and in having Phebe fall in love with a girl disguised as a boy Shakespeare took over from Lodge the typical punishment of the shepherdess who refused the love of the shepherd who adored her in conventional terms.

SOME PASTORAL THEMES

As You Like It, in spite of its carefree tone, is not without its serious themes, for pastoral had traditionally been concerned with philosophical issues, presented usually in the form of a debate. The art-versus-nature theme is embodied most notably in the conflict between the corrupt values of the city from which Duke Senior and his followers have escaped and the values of a country life so pure that even an Oliver must undergo reformation when subjected to its influences. Man living simply in a state of nature cannot long be evil. But there is always Touchstone to argue the case for the court and civilization, and when the problems of the play have been resolved it is to the city that all but Jaques must return. Shakespeare never loses sight of the real world.

Related to this theme is the traditional conflict between Nature and Fortune in the shaping of human destiny. The gifts of the two goddesses are debated by Rosalind and Celia in an important conversation (I.ii.28–52). At the beginning of the play Fortune scorns those whom Nature has favoured; like the fickle goddess which she is, she bestows her favours on the evil Frederick and Oliver, while the good Duke Senior, Rosalind, and Orlando, all endowed by Nature with beauty, wit, and human virtues in their highest forms, must flee to the woods. But at the end of the play the claims of Fortune have been reconciled with those of Nature, for the good, handsome and virtuous are restored to their rightful places of worldly felicity.

Most importantly, the play involves, like all of Shakespeare's comedies, a probing of the nature of love. Orlando, who has been denied proper education by his elder brother, must be educated in the Forest of Arden. He learns there the most important of all social values, that of true love. At the hands of

his teacher, Rosalind, he learns that such Petrarchan protestations as Silvius can express to Phebe are mere outward show —
that "Men have died from time to time, and worms have eaten
them, but not for love" (IV.i.91–2) — and that true love must
be firmly rooted in reality.

TOUCHSTONE AND JAQUES

As You Like It is thus not untouched by the spirit of satire, although O. J. Campbell somewhat overstates the case in *Shakespeare's Satire* (New York: Oxford University Press, 1943), where
he sees the play as primarily a satire directed against the false
pretences of Arcadian romance, and thus a vindication of the
civilized life of cities. Shakespeare knows how to appeal to us
from both points of view. The chief instruments of Shakespeare's
satire are in the witty tongue of Rosalind and in Touchstone
and Jaques, two of his supreme achievements who have no
counterparts in Lodge's romance. Jaques has often been described as the typical Elizabethan malcontent placed in a comic
setting in which he does not belong, but this may be to take
the character too seriously. Little need be added to Kittredge's
description of these characters:

> Jaques and Touchstone, as we have seen, are original with Shake-
> speare. Jaques should not be taken too seriously. He is by no means
> an out-and-out Elizabethan malcontent. If he belongs to that cate-
> gory at all, it is rather in manner than in spirit. He is no cynic,
> and there is no gloom in his melancholy, no sting in his satire.
> He is "wrapped," he tells us, "in a most humorous sadness"
> (IV.i.18), that is, in a pensive cast of mind that indulges in whim-
> sical reflections upon life and manners. That he is fascinated by
> Touchstone and calls for a motley coat is significant in this regard.
> The Duke's arraignment of him as a libertine whose satire would
> corrupt society instead of reforming it (II.vii.64*ff*) is not to be in-
> terpreted literally. "Libertine" meant merely "free-liver," "man of
> the world," and need not be saddled with modern signification.
> The Duke is simply challenging the claim of Jaques to be accepted
> as a promising reformer of society. His object is to put him on the
> defensive, and Jaques accepts the challenge and has the last word.
>   In very truth Jaques and Touchstone (each in his own inimi-

table way) serve a dramatic purpose of the highest order: they act as an unobtrusive chorus, and thus prevent our involving ourselves too deeply in the mists of the purely imaginative. It is largely due to them that we remain aware that the Forest of Arden is not the world, and that Rosalind and Orlando and the Banished Duke are far from home and are all playing their temporary parts in a highly imaginative masquerade and under whimsically unreal conditions. Thus they keep the drama sufficiently aloof from the purely pastoral. "Pastoral-comical" Polonius would term it. Let us add one category to his varied *genres* and call *As You Like It* pastoral-comical-actual. . . .

Touchstone's technique is perfect. Take, for example, the mock-philosophy in his description of a shepherd's life (III.ii.13–21), where the nicely poised antithetical distinctions counterbalance to a hair. Note his punning logic when he proves that Corin is damned, "like an ill-roasted egg," because he has never visited the court. Like Feste and King Lear's fool, Touchstone is a facile rhymster. He has a fine taste in metre, justly scorning the "false gallop" (or canter) of Orlando's verses, which he parodies skillfully. He has addressed love verses of his own to Audrey, but they are beyond her comprehension, and so he compares himself to Ovid among the Goths, with the inevitable pun on "goats." And he has the orthodox Platonic doctrine that all poets are liars. In his encounter with the rustic William, his rival for Audrey's hand (V.i.), he is perhaps most strikingly professional, parading the emptiest truisms with the pomp of philosophic wisdom and the polish of rhetoric. At the same time, we observe, he chastens the Elizabethan exuberance of style in their initial dialogue, which is elegantly simple and quite within William's comprehension. Only in the concluding diatribe does he frolic in verbosity, and here he translates as he goes along.

There is a close sympathetic relation between Touchstone's soliloquy on the lapse of time, as reported by Jaques (II.vii.20–8), and Jaques's own world-weary monologue in the same scene: "All the world's a stage." That man's life is divisible into at least four ages is an observation that must go back to the earliest dawn of intelligence in the human race. Five ages, and ten, are ancient reckonings. Seven — inevitable as a mystic number — is traditionally ascribed to Hippocrates and had become proverbial long before Shakespeare's time. His matchless delineation has established the number in everybody's mind. And who but Jaques could have given the matter so pensively vivid an utterance? Man's life is a drama, and Jaques is the interpretative chorus.

As You Like It

DUKE SENIOR, *living in banishment.*
DUKE FREDERICK, *his brother, and usurper of his dukedom.*
AMIENS,
JAQUES, } *lords attending on the banished* DUKE.
LE BEAU, *a courtier attending on* DUKE FREDERICK.
CHARLES, *wrestler to* DUKE FREDERICK.
OLIVER,
JAQUES DE BOYS, } *sons of* SIR ROWLAND DE BOYS.
ORLANDO,
ADAM,
DENNIS, } *servants to* OLIVER.
TOUCHSTONE, *a clown.*
SIR OLIVER MARTEXT, *a vicar.*
CORIN,
SILVIUS, } *shepherds.*
WILLIAM, *a country fellow, in love with* AUDREY.
HYMEN.

ROSALIND, *daughter to the banished* DUKE.
CELIA, *daughter to* DUKE FREDERICK.
PHEBE, *a shepherdess.*
AUDREY, *a country wench.*

Lords, pages, and attendants, &c.

SCENE. — *Oliver's orchard; Duke Frederick's court;
the Forest of Arden.*]

Act One

<figure>◇◇</figure>

SCENE I. [Oliver's *orchard*.]

Enter Orlando *and* Adam.

ORL.   As I remember, Adam, it was upon this fashion bequeathed me by will but poor a thousand crowns, and,
as thou say'st, charged my brother on his blessing to
breed me well; and there begins my sadness. My brother
Jaques he keeps at school, and report speaks goldenly   5
of his profit. For my part, he keeps me rustically at
home or, to speak more properly, stays me here at home
unkept; for call you that keeping for a gentleman of my
birth that differs not from the stalling of an ox? His
horses are bred better; for, besides that they are fair with   10
their feeding, they are taught their manage, and to that
end riders dearly hir'd; but I, his brother, gain nothing
under him but growth, for the which his animals on his
dunghills are as much bound to him as I. Besides this
nothing that he so plentifully gives me, the something   15
that nature gave me his countenance seems to take from
me. He lets me feed with his hinds, bars me the place of

I.i. 1–2 *fashion bequeathed* F¹; DYCE, K: "fashion: he bequeathed." Various emendations have been proposed in order to supply a subject for "bequeathed." But the
sentence is good idiomatic Elizabethan English without change, and the meaning
is quite obvious. **4** *breed* bring up, educate. **5** *keeps* supports, maintains.
school the university. *goldenly* in golden terms. **6** *profit* proficiency in studies.
keeps me rustically maintains me like a countryman. Orlando puns bitterly on
"keep" in the sense of "detain" [K]. **7** *stays* detains. **8** *unkept* uncared for.
keeping maintenance, support. **9** *stalling* keeping in a stall or stable. **10** *fair*
in good physical condition. **11** *manage* the action and paces through which a
horse is put in training. **16** *his countenance* Either "his behaviour toward me"
or (spoken with bitter irony) "his patronage." Both senses were common [K].
17 *hinds* farm hands.

1

a brother, and, as much as in him lies, mines my gentility with my education. This is it, Adam, that grieves
me; and the spirit of my father, which I think is within   20
me, begins to mutiny against this servitude. I will no
longer endure it, though yet I know no wise remedy how
to avoid it.

Enter Oliver.

ADAM.   Yonder comes my master, your brother.

ORL.   Go apart, Adam, and thou shalt hear how he will shake   25
me up.   [Adam *retires*.]

OLI.   Now, sir, what make you here?

ORL.   Nothing. I am not taught to make anything.

OLI.   What mar you then, sir?

ORL.   Marry, sir, I am helping you to mar that which God   30
made, a poor unworthy brother of yours, with idleness.

OLI.   Marry, sir, be better employed, and be naught awhile!

ORL.   Shall I keep your hogs and eat husks with them? What
prodigal portion have I spent that I should come to such
penury?   35

OLI.   Know you where you are, sir?

ORL.   O, sir, very well. Here in your orchard.

OLI.   Know you before whom, sir?

ORL.   Ay, better than him I am before knows me. I know you
are my eldest brother, and in the gentle condition of   40

18 *mines* undermines.   19 *with* by means of.   *my education* the way in which
I am brought up.   25–6 *shake me up* abuse me violently, berate me.   27 *make
you* are you doing.   29 *What mar you* "Mar" was constantly used in alliterative
antithesis to "make" [K].   30 *Marry* A common interjection, originally an oath
by the Virgin Mary, but used lightly as a mere expletive [K].   32 *be naught
awhile* A common form of curse equivalent to "Go to the mischief" [K].   33 *eat
husks* like the Prodigal Son (LUKE, XV, 16) [K].   33–4 *What prodigal . . . spent*
A condensed form of expression equivalent to "Am I like the Prodigal, who
received his portion and spent it in riotous living?" Orlando's "poor a thousand
crowns," he reminds his brother, allowed no lavish spending, and even that sum
he had not yet received (lines 65–6) [K].   36 *where* in whose presence. Orlando
purposely misinterprets [K].   37 *orchard* garden.   40–1 *and in the gentle . . .
know me* and, as to gentility of race, you ought to regard me in the same way —

blood you should so know me. The courtesy of nations allows you my better in that you are the first born; but the same tradition takes not away my blood, were there twenty brothers betwixt us. I have as much of my father in me as you, albeit I confess your coming before me is 45 nearer to his reverence.

OLI.   What, boy!   [*Strikes him.*]

ORL.   Come, come, elder brother, you are too young in this.

                                              [*Seizes him.*]

OLI.   Wilt thou lay hands on me, villain?

ORL.   I am no villain. I am the youngest son of Sir Rowland 50 de Boys; he was my father, and he is thrice a villain that says such a father begot villains. Wert thou not my brother, I would not take this hand from thy throat till this other had pull'd out thy tongue for saying so. Thou hast rail'd on thyself.   55

ADAM. [*comes forward*] Sweet masters, be patient! For your father's remembrance, be at accord!

OLI.   Let me go, I say.

ORL.   I will not till I please. You shall hear me. My father charg'd you in his will to give me good education. You 60 have train'd me like a peasant, obscuring and hiding from me all gentlemanlike qualities. The spirit of my father grows strong in me, and I will no longer endure it. Therefore allow me such exercises as may become a

---

that is, acknowledge me as a brother and not think me your inferior [K].   41 *The courtesy of nations* the polite conventions of the world. These, Orlando declares, are mere matters of traditional custom; they have nothing to do with nature. The injustice of the privileges attached to primogeniture is exposed by Edmund in his matchless soliloquy in KING LEAR (I.II.2–6) [K].   45–6 *is nearer to his reverence* entitles you to more of the respect due to a father [K].   48 *you are too young* you act too much like a hot-headed youngster [K].   49 *villain* Orlando takes the word in the sense of "serf," its original meaning.   56 *Sweet* beloved. 59 *I will not till I please* The ease with which Orlando, the "boy" holds his elder brother in spite of his struggling, prepares us for his prowess against Charles the wrestler [K].   62 *qualities* accomplishments.   64 *exercises* activities. *become* be fitting for.

gentleman, or give me the poor allottery my father left 65
me by testament. With that I will go buy my fortunes.

[*Releases him.*]

OLI.   And what wilt thou do? beg when that is spent? Well,
sir, get you in. I will not long be troubled with you.
You shall have some part of your will. I pray you leave
me.   70

ORL.   I will no further offend you than becomes me for my
good.

OLI.   Get you with him, you old dog!

ADAM.   Is "old dog" my reward? Most true, I have lost my teeth
in your service. God be with my old master! he would 75
not have spoke such a word.   *Exeunt* Orlando, Adam.

OLI.   Is it even so? Begin you to grow upon me? I will physic
your rankness, and yet give no thousand crowns neither.
Holla, Dennis!

Enter Dennis.

DEN.   Calls your worship?   80

OLI.   Was not Charles the Duke's wrestler here to speak with
me?

DEN.   So please you, he is here at the door and importunes
access to you.

OLI.   Call him in. [*Exit* Dennis.] 'Twill be a good way; and 85
to-morrow the wrestling is.

Enter Charles.

---

65 *allottery* allotment, portion.   77 *to grow upon me* to become so big that you occupy more than your due space in the world and so crowd me — encroach upon my rights and privileges. The figure is continued in "rankness" (i.e. overgrowth) [K]. *physic* reduce, as by medical treatment [K].   78 *no . . . neither* Such double negatives are common in Shakespeare [K].   99 *that she* F³; F¹: "that hec."   100 *to stay* if she had been forced to stay.   105 *Forest of Arden* Shakespeare follows Lodge in laying the scene in "the Forest of Arden," that is, Ardennes, on the Meuse; but no doubt he remembered the Forest of Arden in Warwickshire, his native county [K]. Shakespeare is not concerned with specific geography, for

CHA.   Good morrow to your worship.

OLI.   Good Monsieur Charles! What's the new news at the
         new court?

CHA.   There's no news at the court, sir, but the old news.   90
         That is, the old Duke is banished by his younger brother
         the new Duke, and three or four loving lords have put
         themselves into voluntary exile with him, whose lands
         and revenues enrich the new Duke; therefore he gives
         them good leave to wander.   95

OLI.   Can you tell if Rosalind, the Duke's daughter, be ban-
         ished with her father?

CHA.   O, no! for the Duke's daughter her cousin so loves her,
         being ever from their cradles bred together, that she
         would have followed her exile, or have died to stay be- 100
         hind her. She is at the court, and no less beloved of her
         uncle than his own daughter, and never two ladies loved
         as they do.

OLI.   Where will the old Duke live?

CHA.   They say he is already in the Forest of Arden, and a   105
         many merry men with him; and there they live like the
         old Robin Hood of England. They say many young
         gentlemen flock to him every day, and fleet the time
         carelessly as they did in the golden world.

OLI.   What, you wrestle to-morrow before the new Duke?   110

CHA.   Marry do I, sir; and I came to acquaint you with a
         matter. I am given, sir, secretly to understand that your
         younger brother, Orlando, hath a disposition to come in
         disguis'd against me to try a fall. To-morrow, sir, I

what he is giving us is the imaginary forest of pastoral literature.   107 *Robin
Hood* Ballads about Robin Hood go back to at least the end of the fourteenth
century and were widely popular in Shakespeare's time. He appeared as a
character in May games and in folk drama as well as upon the public stage.
108 *fleet the time* make the time float by [K]   109 *in the golden world* in the
Golden Age, when there was neither toil nor trouble [K]. The division of the
history of the world into four ages goes back to classical antiquity. The later
ages of Silver, Bronze, and Iron had supposedly witnessed a progressive deteriora-
tion of man and society.   114 *fall* wrestling bout.

wrestle for my credit, and he that escapes me without 115
some broken limb shall acquit him well. Your brother
is but young and tender, and for your love I would be
loath to foil him, as I must for my own honour if he
come in. Therefore, out of my love to you, I came
hither to acquaint you withal, that either you might 120
stay him from his intendment, or brook such disgrace
well as he shall run into, in that it is a thing of his own
search and altogether against my will.

OLI.   Charles, I thank thee for thy love to me, which thou
shalt find I will most kindly requite. I had myself notice 125
of my brother's purpose herein and have by underhand
means laboured to dissuade him from it; but he is resolute. I'll tell thee, Charles, it is the stubbornest young
fellow of France; full of ambition, an envious emulator
of every man's good parts, a secret and villainous con- 130
triver against me his natural brother. Therefore use thy
discretion. I had as lief thou didst break his neck as his
finger. And thou wert best look to't; for if thou dost
him any slight disgrace, or if he do not mightily grace
himself on thee, he will practise against thee by poison, 135
entrap thee by some treacherous device, and never leave
thee till he hath ta'en thy life by some indirect means
or other; for I assure thee (and almost with tears I speak
it) there is not one so young and so villainous this day
living. I speak but brotherly of him; but should I anat- 140
omize him to thee as he is, I must blush and weep, and
thou must look pale and wonder.

CHA.   I am heartily glad I came hither to you. If he come to-
morrow, I'll give him his payment. If ever he go alone

---

115 *for my credit* to enhance my reputation.   118 *to foil him* to defeat him —
that is, when defeat implies serious injury [ᴋ].   120 *withal* with this fact.   121
stay . . . intendment prevent him from fulfilling his intention.   121–2 *brook
. . . well* put up with.   126–7 *by underhand means* Oliver implies that Orlando
is too headstrong to listen to direct expostulation [ᴋ].   129 *envious emulator*
malicious rival.   130 *parts* accomplishments.   131 *natural* by birth.   132 *I had
as lief* it would be as agreeable to me.   134–5 *grace himself* win honour to himself.   135 *practise* plot, deal treacherously.   137 *indirect* circuitous, underhand.
140 *but brotherly* less than the truth about him, as befits a brother [ᴋ].   140–1
anatomize dissect (in the figurative sense).   142 *look pale* with horror at the

again, I'll never wrestle for prize more. And so God 145
keep your worship!

OLI.   Farewell, good Charles. *Exit* [Charles]. Now will I stir
this gamester. I hope I shall see an end of him; for my
soul (yet I know not why) hates nothing more than he.
Yet he's gentle; never school'd and yet learned; full of 150
noble device; of all sorts enchantingly beloved, and indeed so much in the heart of the world, and especially
of my own people, who best know him, that I am altogether misprised. But it shall not be so long; this wrestler
shall clear all. Nothing remains but that I kindle the 155
boy thither, which now I'll go about.   *Exit.*

◇◇◇◇◇◇◇◇◇◇◇◇◇◇◇◇◇◇

S C E N E   I I.
[*A lawn before* Duke Frederick's *Palace.*]

Enter Rosalind *and* Celia.

CEL.   I pray thee, Rosalind, sweet my coz, be merry.

ROS.   Dear Celia, I show more mirth than I am mistress of,
and would you yet I were merrier? Unless you could
teach me to forget a banished father, you must not learn
me how to remember any extraordinary pleasure.   5

CEL.   Herein I see thou lov'st me not with the full weight that
I love thee. If my uncle, thy banished father, had banished thy uncle, the Duke my father, so thou hadst been
still with me, I could have taught my love to take thy
father for mine. So wouldst thou, if the truth of thy love 10

---

thought of making an enemy of such a man [K].   144 *go alone* walk without
crutches.   146 *keep* protect.   147 *Oli* F²; not in F¹.   *stir* incite (to wrestle).
148 *gamester* (a) athlete, sportsman (b) merry, gamesome fellow.   150 *gentle*
furnished with all the qualities that befit a gentleman [K].   151 *device* ideas.
enchantingly as if by enchantment. An allusion to the old belief that affection
could be won by magic spells and potions [K].   154 *misprised* undervalued,
scorned.   155 *clear all* settle everything.   156 *thither* to the westling match.   *go
about* attend to.

I.II. 1 *coz* cousin.   3 *yet I were* ROWE; F¹: "were."   4 *learn* teach.   8 *so* provided that.   10 *truth* true substance.

to me were so righteously temper'd as mine is to thee.

ROS. Well, I will forget the condition of my estate to rejoice in yours.

CEL. You know my father hath no child but I, nor none is like to have; and truly, when he dies, thou shalt be his 15 heir; for what he hath taken away from thy father perforce, I will render thee again in affection. By mine honour, I will! and when I break that oath, let me turn monster. Therefore, my sweet Rose, my dear Rose, be merry. 20

ROS. From henceforth I will, coz, and devise sports. Let me see. What think you of falling in love?

CEL. Marry, I prithee do, to make sport withal! But love no man in good earnest, nor no further in sport neither than with safety of a pure blush thou mayst in honour 25 come off again.

ROS. What shall be our sport then?

CEL. Let us sit and mock the good housewife Fortune from her wheel, that her gifts may henceforth be bestowed equally. 30

ROS. I would we could do so; for her benefits are mightily misplaced, and the bountiful blind woman doth most mistake in her gifts to women.

CEL. 'Tis true; for those that she makes fair she scarce makes honest, and those that she makes honest she makes very 35 ill-favouredly.

ROS. Nay, now thou goest from Fortune's office to Nature's.

---

11 *righteously temper'd* properly composed; composed of the right elements [K]. 12 *estate* circumstances in life. 16–17 *perforce* by force. 17 *render thee again* pay thee back. 23 *withal* therewith. 25 *with safety . . . in honour* honourably and in safety, so that your blushes may still be those of modesty and not of shame [K]. 26 *come off* escape. 28 *good housewife Fortune* In calling Fortune a "housewife," Celia doubtless had in mind the two meanings of that word: (a) the woman of the house, with her spinning wheel (b) the "hussy" who grants favours to all men but is constant to none [K]. The wheel of Fortune is a constant motif of classical and medieval literature. 35 *honest* chaste. 36 *ill-favouredly* harshfeatured, ugly. 37 *office* duty, proper function. 38–9 *Fortune reigns . . . of*

Fortune reigns in gifts of the world, not in the lineaments of Nature.

Enter [Touchstone, the] Clown.

CEL.   No? When Nature hath made a fair creature, may she   40
not by Fortune fall into the fire? Though Nature hath
given us wit to flout at Fortune, hath not Fortune sent
in this fool to cut off the argument?

ROS.   Indeed, there is Fortune too hard for Nature when
Fortune makes Nature's natural the cutter-off of Na-   45
ture's wit.

CEL.   Peradventure this is not Fortune's work neither, but
Nature's; who perceiveth our natural wits too dull to
reason of such goddesses and hath sent this natural for
our whetstone, for always the dulness of the fool is the   50
whetstone of the wits. How now, wit? Whither wander
you?

TOUCH. Mistress, you must come away to your father.

CEL.   Were you made the messenger?

TOUCH. · No, by mine honour; but I was bid to come for you.   55

ROS.   Where learned you that oath, fool?

TOUCH. Of a certain knight that swore by his honour they were
good pancakes, and swore by his honour the mustard
was naught. Now I'll stand to it, the pancakes were
naught, and the mustard was good, and yet was not the   60
knight forsworn.

Nature This is an ancient idea, going back to Seneca: Nature grants men their
beauty and wit, Fortune their money, wealth, power, etc., in relation to their
fellow men.   42 *wit to flout at Fortune* cleverness which enables us to jeer
at Fortune. Cf. what Jaques says about Touchstone's "railing at Lady Fortune"
(II.vii.12–19) [K].   43 *argument* discussion.   45 *natural* born fool, idiot — but the
term was often applied to professional jesters as well.   47 *Peradventure* perhaps.
51–2 *Whither wander you* "Wit, whither wilt?" (i.e. "Whither wilt thou go, my
wits?") was a common saying, used jocosely to suggest that one's thoughts were
wandering [K].   59 *naught* worthless.   61 *forsworn* a liar, having sworn falsely.

CEL.   How prove you that in the great heap of your knowl-
         edge?

ROS.   Ay, marry, now unmuzzle your wisdom.

TOUCH.   Stand you both forth now. Stroke your chins, and swear   65
         by your beards that I am a knave.

CEL.   By our beards (if we had them), thou art.

TOUCH.   By my knavery (if I had it), then I were. But if you
         swear by that that is not, you are not forsworn. No
         more was this knight, swearing by his honour, for he   70
         never had any; or if he had, he had sworn it away be-
         fore ever he saw those pancakes or that mustard.

CEL.   Prithee, who is't that thou mean'st?

TOUCH.   One that old Frederick, your father, loves.

CEL.   My father's love is enough to honour him. Enough!   75
         Speak no more of him. You'll be whipp'd for taxation
         one of these days.

TOUCH.   The more pity that fools may not speak wisely what
         wise men do foolishly.

CEL.   By my troth, thou sayest true; for, since the little wit 80
         that fools have was silenced, the little foolery that wise
         men have makes a great show. Here comes Monsieur
         Le Beau.

                         Enter Le Beau.

ROS.   With his mouth full of news.

---

68 *By my knavery* Intentionally ambiguous. In its first meaning it is an oath which
is no oath, like "by our beards," because it is made by something that does not
exist. Its second meaning is "by means of," "by reason of my knavery" [K].   72
pancakes flapjacks or fritters made with meat and thus to be eaten with mustard.
75 *Cel* THEOBALD; F¹: "Ros."   76 *taxation* satirical criticism.   78 *The more pity*
The conversation of stage fools frequently turns on this antithesis: the folly of
those who have their wits and the wisdom of fools [K].   81 *was silenced* The court
of Rosalind's father, at which Touchstone's wit had been relished, was more favourable to frankness than that of the suspicious usurper Frederick. This speech, with
Celia's friendly warning to the fool, gives us a hint of what to expect from Duke
Frederick when he appears [K].   85 *put on* force upon.   87 *more marketable*
Poulterers often stuffed birds before killing them in order to increase their weight.
90 *colour* sort. Cf. III.ii.384. Celia speaks in a slightly affected style for the sake

CEL.	Which he will put on us as pigeons feed their young. 85
ROS.	Then shall we be news-cramm'd.
CEL.	All the better! We shall be the more marketable. — Bon jour, Monsieur Le Beau. What's the news?
LE BEAU.	Fair princess, you have lost much good sport.
CEL.	Sport? of what colour? 90
LE BEAU.	What colour, madam? How shall I answer you?
ROS.	As wit and fortune will.
TOUCH.	Or as the Destinies decree.
CEL.	Well said! That was laid on with a trowel.
TOUCH.	Nay, if I keep not my rank — 95
ROS.	Thou losest thy old smell.
LE BEAU.	You amaze me, ladies. I would have told you of good wrestling, which you have lost the sight of.
ROS.	Yet tell us the manner of the wrestling.
LE BEAU.	I will tell you the beginning; and if it please your lady- 100 ships, you may see the end; for the best is yet to do; and here, where you are, they are coming to perform it.
CEL.	Well, the beginning that is dead and buried.
LE BEAU.	There comes an old man and his three sons —
CEL.	I could match this beginning with an old tale. 105
LE BEAU.	Three proper young men, of excellent growth and presence.

---

of disconcerting Le Beau. He is confused, for he is rather literal-minded and cannot think of any actual colour that would fitly describe the sport of wrestling [K]. 92 *As wit and fortune will* The suggestion is that Le Beau's wits are slow and need the aid of good luck to furnish a clever reply [K].   93 *decree* POPE; F¹: "decrees."   94 *laid on with a trowel* said very bluntly (as a mason slaps down mortar).   95 *rank* position (as a first-rate jester). Rosalind puns on the word. 97 *amaze* perplex, confuse.   101 *to do* to be done.   105 *an old tale* Le Beau's story begins, as every one must see, like a nursery tale with its inevitable three adventurers. The incident of the old man and his two sons is adapted from Lodge [K].   106 *proper* handsome.   106–7 *presence* bearing. Rosalind ridicules Le Beau's pompous style by punning on the word; she recites the formal opening of a proclamation.

ROS.   With bills on their necks, "Be it known unto all men by
these presents" —

LE BEAU.   The eldest of the three wrestled with Charles, the Duke's 110
wrestler; which Charles in a moment threw him and
broke three of his ribs, that there is little hope of life in
him. So he serv'd the second, and so the third. Yonder
they lie, the poor old man, their father, making such
pitiful dole over them that all the beholders take his 115
part with weeping.

ROS.   Alas!

TOUCH.   But what is the sport, monsieur, that the ladies have
lost?

LE BEAU.   Why, this that I speak of.   120

TOUCH.   Thus men may grow wiser every day. It is the first time
that ever I heard breaking of ribs was sport for ladies.

CEL.   Or I, I promise thee.

ROS.   But is there any else longs to see this broken music in his
sides? Is there yet another dotes upon rib-breaking? Shall 125
we see this wrestling, cousin?

LE BEAU.   You must, if you stay here; for here is the place ap-
pointed for the wrestling and they are ready to perform
it.

CEL.   Yonder sure they are coming. Let us now stay and see it. 130

Flourish. Enter Duke [Frederick],
Lords, Orlando, Charles, *and* Attendants.

DUKE.   Come on. Since the youth will not be entreated, his own
peril on his forwardness!

---

108 *bills* (a) documents (b) long pointed weapons with hooks near their ends.   115
dole lamentation.   124–5 *to see . . . sides* to see his ribs broken. "Broken music"
means, literally, music arranged in parts for several distinct instruments [K].
131–2 *his own . . . forwardness* let him run the risk of his own rashness.   135
successfully as if he might succeed.   140 *odds* disparity.   *the men* HANMER; F¹:
"the man."   146 *them* As Orlando approaches the two ladies, who appear to be of

ROS.   Is yonder the man?

LE BEAU. Even he, madam.

CEL.   Alas, he is too young! Yet he looks successfully.   135

DUKE. How now, daughter, and cousin! Are you crept hither to see the wrestling?

ROS.   Ay, my liege, so please you give us leave.

DUKE. You will take little delight in it, I can tell you, there is such odds in the men. In pity of the challenger's youth 140 I would fain dissuade him, but he will not be entreated. Speak to him, ladies; see if you can move him.

CEL.   Call him hither, good Monsieur Le Beau.

DUKE. Do so. I'll not be by.   [*Steps aside.*]

LE BEAU. Monsieur the challenger, the princess calls for you.   145

ORL.   I attend them with all respect and duty.

ROS.   Young man, have you challeng'd Charles the wrestler?

ORL.   No, fair princess. He is the general challenger; I come but in as others do, to try with him the strength of my youth.   150

CEL.   Young gentleman, your spirits are too bold for your years. You have seen cruel proof of this man's strength. If you saw yourself with your eyes, or knew yourself with your judgment, the fear of your adventure would counsel you to a more equal enterprise. We pray you for 155 your own sake to embrace your own safety and give over this attempt.

ROS.   Do, young sir. Your reputation shall not therefore be misprised. We will make it our suit to the Duke that the wrestling might not go forward.   160

---

equal rank, he includes them both in his reply, especially since he does not know which is which (line 242). Here, as always, Shakespeare wrote with the stage action in mind [K].   153 *If you saw . . . eyes* if you would use your own eyes to see. 153-4 *knew yourself . . . judgment* used your own judgment to evaluate yourself. 159 *misprised* undervalued. A mild word for "disgraced" [K].

ORL.   I beseech you, punish me not with your hard thoughts,
       wherein I confess me much guilty to deny so fair and
       excellent ladies anything. But let your fair eyes and
       gentle wishes go with me to my trial; wherein if I be
       foil'd, there is but one sham'd that was never gracious; 165
       if kill'd, but one dead that is willing to be so. I shall do
       my friends no wrong, for I have none to lament me; the
       world no injury, for in it I have nothing. Only in the
       world I fill up a place, which may be better supplied
       when I have made it empty.   170

ROS.   The little strength that I have, I would it were with you.

CEL.   And mine, to eke out hers.

ROS.   Fare you well. Pray heaven I be deceiv'd in you!

CEL.   Your heart's desires be with you!

CHA.   Come, where is this young gallant that is so desirous to 175
       lie with his mother earth?

ORL.   Ready, sir; but his will hath in it a more modest work-
       ing.

DUKE. You shall try but one fall.

CHA.   No, I warrant your Grace you shall not entreat him to 180
       a second that have so mightily persuaded him from a
       first.

ORL.   You mean to mock me after. You should not have
       mock'd me before. But come your ways!

ROS.   Now Hercules be thy speed, young man!   185

CEL.   I would I were invisible, to catch the strong fellow by
       the leg.   *Wrestle.*

ROS.   O excellent young man!

161–3 *punish me not . . . anything* punish me not by thinking ill of me in respect
to that in which I confess I am blameworthy, namely in refusing so fair and excellent ladies anything [K].   163–4 *fair eyes and gentle wishes* In antithesis to "hard
thoughts" (line 161). "Fair eyes" combines both the obvious sense and that of
"favourable looks," such as they would not give him if they entertained hard
thoughts [K].   165 *foil'd* disgracefully beaten. *gracious* honoured; regarded with

CEL.   If I had a thunderbolt in mine eye, I can tell who
        should down.   [*Charles is thrown.*] *Shout.* 190

DUKE.   No more, no more!

ORL.   Yes, I beseech your Grace. I am not yet well breath'd.

DUKE.   How dost thou, Charles?

LE BEAU.   He cannot speak, my lord.

DUKE.   Bear him away.   [*Charles is borne out.*]
                What is thy name, young man?

ORL.   Orlando, my liege, the youngest son of Sir Rowland de 195
        Boys.

DUKE.   I would thou hadst been son to some man else!
        The world esteem'd thy father honourable,
        But I did find him still mine enemy.
        Thou shouldst have better pleas'd me with this deed,   200
        Hadst thou descended from another house.
        But fare thee well; thou art a gallant youth;
        I would thou hadst told me of another father.

                Exeunt Duke, [Train, *and* Le Beau].

CEL.   Were I my father, coz, would I do this?

ORL.   I am more proud to be Sir Rowland's son,   205
        His youngest son, and would not change that calling
        To be adopted heir to Frederick.

ROS.   My father lov'd Sir Rowland as his soul,
        And all the world was of my father's mind.
        Had I before known this young man his son,   210
        I should have given him tears unto entreaties
        Ere he should thus have ventur'd.

CEL.   Gentle cousin,

---

favour [K].   173 *deceiv'd in you* i.e. in so far as your ability as a wrestler is concerned.   177–8 *modest working* moderate operation [K].   185 *speed* helper to suc-
cess [K].   192 *I am not yet well breath'd* I have not yet exerted myself sufficiently
to make it good exercise for me [K]. To "breathe" is "to take exercise."   199
still always.   206 *calling* title. He would rather be a mere younger son of Sir Rowland than heir of Duke Frederick.   211 *unto* in addition to.

Let us go thank him and encourage him.
My father's rough and envious disposition
Sticks me at heart. Sir, you have well deserv'd.　　215
If you do keep your promises in love
But justly as you have exceeded all promise,
Your mistress shall be happy.

ROS.　　　　　　　　　　　Gentleman,

　　　　　　[Gives him a chain from her neck.]

Wear this for me, one out of suits with Fortune,
That could give more but that her hand lacks means.　　220
Shall we go, coz?

CEL.　　　　　　　　Ay. Fare you well, fair gentleman.

ORL.　　Can I not say "I thank you"? My better parts
Are all thrown down, and that which here stands up
Is but a quintain, a mere lifeless block.

ROS.　　He calls us back. My pride fell with my fortunes;　　225
I'll ask him what he would. Did you call, sir?
Sir, you have wrestled well, and overthrown
More than your enemies.

CEL.　　　　　　　　　Will you go, coz?

ROS.　　Have with you. Fare you well.

　　　　　　　　Exeunt [Rosalind *and* Celia].

ORL.　　What passion hangs these weights upon my tongue?　　230
I cannot speak to her, yet she urg'd conference.

---

214 *envious* malicious.　　215 *Sticks me at heart* stabs me at the heart; is a stab in my heart. To "stick" in the sense of "stab" was formerly a dignified word [K]. 216-17 *If you do keep . . . all promise* if you only keep your love promises with an exactness comparable to the degree in which you have surpassed all promise (i.e. expectation) in this wrestling match [K].　　218 *mistress* sweetheart.　　219 *one out of suits with Fortune* one to whose suits Fortune pays no heed. The figure is that of a courtier in disfavour [K]. There may be a pun on "suits" in the sense of "livery," the uniform which a dismissed servant would have to give up.　　220 *could* would gladly.　　222 *better parts* mind and spirit.　　224 *quintain* an apparatus for practice in tilting. It was a tall post with a crossbar near the top so adjusted as to swing freely in a circle. At one end the bar broadened into a flat shieldlike surface; at the other end there hung a bag of sand. The tilter aimed to hit the shield fairly

Enter Le Beau.

O poor Orlando, thou art overthrown!
Or Charles or something weaker masters thee.

LE BEAU. Good sir, I do in friendship counsel you
To leave this place. Albeit you have deserv'd   235
High commendation, true applause, and love,
Yet such is now the Duke's condition
That he misconsters all that you have done.
The Duke is humorous. What he is, indeed,
More suits you to conceive than I to speak of.   240

ORL.   I thank you, sir: and pray you tell me this —
Which of the two was daughter of the Duke,
That here was at the wrestling?

LE BEAU. Neither his daughter, if we judge by manners;
But yet indeed the smaller is his daughter;   245
The other is daughter to the banish'd Duke,
And here detain'd by her usurping uncle
To keep his daughter company, whose loves
Are dearer than the natural bond of sisters.
But I can tell you that of late this Duke   250
Hath ta'en displeasure 'gainst his gentle niece,
Grounded upon no other argument
But that the people praise her for her virtues
And pity her for her good father's sake;
And, on my life, his malice 'gainst the lady   255
Will suddenly break forth. Sir, fare you well.

---

with the point of his lance [K].   227-8 *overthrown . . . enemies* He has won her
heart as well as the wrestling match.   229 *Have with you* An idiomatic expression
of readiness to accompany a person [K].   231 *urg'd conference* invited conversation.   233 *Or* either.   237 *condition* disposition.   238 *misconsters* misconstrues,
misinterprets.   239 *humorous* capricious, notional, full of whims and impulses
[K].   244 *manners* character and disposition (like the Latin "mores") [K].   245
smaller MALONE; F¹: "taller." That Celia is the smaller of the two girls is clearly
established at I.III.110, III.V.117, and IV.III.87.   248 *whose loves* whose love for
each other. Such abstract nouns are often pluralized in Elizabethan English when
more than one person is thought of [K].   252 *argument* cause.   256 *suddenly*
soon.

Hereafter, in a better world than this,
I shall desire more love and knowledge of you.

ORL   I rest much bounden to you. Fare you well.

                        [*Exit* Le Beau.]

Thus must I from the smoke into the smother,   260
From tyrant Duke unto a tyrant brother.
But heavenly Rosalind!   *Exit.*

◇◇◇◇◇◇◇◇◇◇◇◇◇◇◇◇◇

SCENE III. [*A room in the* Duke's *Palace.*]

Enter Celia *and* Rosalind.

CEL.   Why, cousin! why, Rosalind! Cupid have mercy! not a
        word?

ROS.   Not one to throw at a dog.

CEL.   No, thy words are too precious to be cast away upon
        curs; throw some of them at me. Come, lame me with   5
        reasons.

ROS.   Then there were two cousins laid up, when the one
        should be lam'd with reasons, and the other mad without
        any.

CEL.   But is all this for your father?   10

ROS.   No, some of it is for my child's father. O, how full of
        briers is this working-day world!

---

257 *in a better world* under better conditions; in a better time.   259 *bounden*
obliged.   260 *must I* I am forced.   *from . . . smother* A proverbial phrase like
"out of the frying pan into the fire" [ᴋ].
    I.III. 1 *Cupid have mercy* Jestingly (but significantly) substituted for "God have
mercy," in accordance with the old literary and social convention (seen frequently
in Chaucer and the medieval writers) which elevates Cupid or Love to the position
of a deity whom lovers honour in due form [ᴋ].   5–6 *lame me with reasons* injure
me with words, talk.   8 *mad* i.e. (merely) melancholy [ᴋ].   11 *child's father* fu-
ture husband.   13–14 *holiday foolery* as opposed to "this working-day world."   18
Hem them away get rid of them by saying "hem," i.e. clearing your throat.   19

CEL.   They are but burrs, cousin, thrown upon thee in holi-
       day foolery. If we walk not in the trodden paths, our
       very petticoats will catch them.   15

ROS.   I could shake them off my coat. These burrs are in my
       heart.

CEL.   Hem them away.

ROS.   I would try, if I could cry "hem!" and have him.

CEL.   Come, come, wrestle with thy affections.   20

ROS.   O, they take the part of a better wrestler than myself!

CEL.   O, a good wish upon you! You will try in time, in de-
       spite of a fall. But, turning these jests out of service, let
       us talk in good earnest. Is it possible on such a sudden
       you should fall into so strong a liking with old Sir Row- 25
       land's youngest son?

ROS.   The Duke my father lov'd his father dearly.

CEL.   Doth it therefore ensue that you should love his son
       dearly? By this kind of chase, I should hate him, for my
       father hated his father dearly; yet I hate not Orlando.   30

ROS.   No, faith, hate him not, for my sake!

CEL.   Why should I not? Doth he not deserve well?

                   Enter Duke [Frederick], *with* Lords.

ROS.   Let me love him for that; and do you love him because
       I do. Look, here comes the Duke.

CEL.   With his eyes full of anger.   35

DUKE. Mistress, dispatch you with your safest haste

---

cry . . . him have him with such slight effort (with the obvious play on words).
20 *affections* feelings, emotions.   **22** *try* make trial (at wrestling). Some editors
would read "cry" and take "cry in time" as a reference to the nine months of
childbirth. "Fall" would thus have a meaning in addition to "a fall at wrestling."
despite spite.   **28** *ensue* follow logically.   **29** *By this kind of chase* by this violent
way of pursuing an argument [K].   **30** *dearly* intensely.   **32** *deserve well* fully
merit (my hatred). Rosalind takes the expression to mean "to be a deserving or
meritorious person."   **36** *with your safest haste* The implication is, "The more
haste you make, the safer you will be" [K].

And get you from our court!

ROS.   Me, uncle?

DUKE.   You, cousin.
Within these ten days if that thou beest found
So near our public court as twenty miles,
Thou diest for it.

ROS.   I do beseech your Grace   40
Let me the knowledge of my fault bear with me.
If with myself I hold intelligence
Or have acquaintance with mine own desires;
If that I do not dream or be not frantic,
As I do trust I am not — then, dear uncle,   45
Never so much as in a thought unborn
Did I offend your Highness.

DUKE.   Thus do all traitors.
If their purgation did consist in words,
They are as innocent as grace itself.
Let it suffice thee that I trust thee not.   50

ROS.   Yet your mistrust cannot make me a traitor.
Tell me whereon the likelihood depends.

DUKE.   Thou art thy father's daughter. There's enough!

ROS.   So was I when your Highness took his dukedom;
So was I when your Highness banish'd him.   55
Treason is not inherited, my lord;
Or if we did derive it from our friends,
What's that to me? My father was no traitor.
Then, good my liege, mistake me not so much
To think my poverty is treacherous.   60

CEL.   Dear sovereign, hear me speak.

DUKE.   Ay, Celia. We stay'd her for your sake,

---

42 *hold intelligence* am in communication.   44 *frantic* raving mad.   48 *purgation* exculpation, proof of innocence.   49 *grace* virtue.   52 *likelihood* suspicion (F²; F¹: "likelihoods").   57 *friends* relatives.   62 *stay'd* kept (at court).   65 *remorse* compassion.   68 *still* always.   70 *Juno's swans* Swans were birds sacred to Venus; peacocks were the birds traditionally associated with Juno.   72 *subtile* subtle,

Else had she with her father rang'd along.

CEL.   I did not then entreat to have her stay;
       It was your pleasure and your own remorse.   65
       I was too young that time to value her;
       But now I know her. If she be a traitor,
       Why, so am I! We still have slept together,
       Rose at an instant, learn'd, play'd, eat together;
       And wheresoe'er we went, like Juno's swans,   70
       Still we went coupled and inseparable.

DUKE. She is too subtile for thee; and her smoothness,
       Her very silence and her patience,
       Speak to the people, and they pity her.
       Thou art a fool. She robs thee of thy name,   75
       And thou wilt show more bright and seem more virtuous
       When she is gone. Then open not thy lips.
       Firm and irrevocable is my doom
       Which I have pass'd upon her. She is banish'd.

CEL.   Pronounce that sentence then on me, my liege!   80
       I cannot live out of her company.

DUKE. You are a fool. You, niece, provide yourself.
       If you outstay the time, upon mine honour,
       And in the greatness of my word, you die.

                              Exeunt Duke &c.

CEL.   O my poor Rosalind! whither wilt thou go?   85
       Wilt thou change fathers? I will give thee mine.
       I charge thee be not thou more griev'd than I am.

ROS.   I have more cause.

CEL.   Thou hast not, cousin.
       Prithee be cheerful. Know'st thou not the Duke

---

crafty.   73 *patience* calm acceptance of misfortune.   75 *name* reputation.   76
show appear. *virtuous* full of good qualities and accomplishments.   78 *doom*
judgment, sentence.   84 *in the greatness of my word* on my word as a sovereign.
"In" is common in asseverations and appeals [K].   86 *change* exchange.

Hath banish'd me, his daughter?

ROS.   That he hath not!   90

CEL. No? hath not? Rosalind lacks then the love
Which teacheth thee that thou and I am one.
Shall we be sund'red? shall we part, sweet girl?
No! let my father seek another heir.
Therefore devise with me how we may fly,   95
Whither to go, and what to bear with us.
And do not seek to take your change upon you,
To bear your griefs yourself and leave me out;
For, by this heaven, now at our sorrows pale,
Say what thou canst, I'll go along with thee!   100

ROS. Why, whither shall we go?

CEL. To seek my uncle in the Forest of Arden.

ROS. Alas, what danger will it be to us,
Maids as we are, to travel forth so far!
Beauty provoketh thieves sooner than gold.   105

CEL. I'll put myself in poor and mean attire
And with a kind of umber smirch my face;
The like do you. So shall we pass along
And never stir assailants.

ROS.   Were it not better,
Because that I am more than common tall,   110
That I did suit me all points like a man?
A gallant curtleaxe upon my thigh,
A boar-spear in my hand, and — in my heart
Lie there what hidden woman's fear there will —
We'll have a swashing and a martial outside,   115
As many other mannish cowards have
That do outface it with their semblances.

CEL. What shall I call thee when thou art a man?

---

90 *Hath banish'd me* In Lodge the King banishes both Rosalind and his daughter
[K].   92 *thee* F¹; THEOBALD, K: "me."   97 *change* i.e. of fortune (F¹; F², K: "charge,"
meaning "burden of troubles").   107 *umber* brown earth.   109 *stir* incite.   111
suit me all points dress myself in all respects.   112 *curtleaxe* cutlass, short curved
sword.   115 *swashing* swaggering.   117 *outface it* face it out; carry all before

ROS.   I'll have no worse a name than Jove's own page,
        And therefore look you call me Ganymede.   120
        But what will you be call'd?

CEL.   Something that hath a reference to my state —
        No longer Celia, but Aliena.

ROS.   But, cousin, what if we assay'd to steal
        The clownish fool out of your father's court?   125
        Would he not be a comfort to our travel?

CEL.   He'll go along o'er the wide world with me.
        Leave me alone to woo him. Let's away
        And get our jewels and our wealth together,
        Devise the fittest time and safest way   130
        To hide us from pursuit that will be made
        After my flight. Now go in we content
        To liberty, and not to banishment.   *Exeunt.*

---

them; swagger with bravado. To "outface" a person is to daunt or subdue him by
one's resolute bearing [K]. *semblances* false appearances.   120 *Ganymede* the
boy whose beauty led Jove to make him his cupbearer.   122 *my state* my condition (as one alienated from my family) [K].   124 *assay'd* undertook.   128 *woo*
coax.   132 *in we* F¹; F², K: "we in."

Act Two

SCENE I.
[*The Forest of Arden. Before* Duke Senior's *cave.*]

Enter Duke Senior, Amiens, *and two or three* Lords, *like* Foresters.

DUKE S. Now, my co-mates and brothers in exile,
Hath not old custom made this life more sweet
Than that of painted pomp? Are not these woods
More free from peril than the envious court?
Here feel we not the penalty of Adam,   5
The seasons' difference; as, the icy fang
And churlish chiding of the winter's wind,
Which, when it bites and blows upon my body
Even till I shrink with cold, I smile, and say
"This is no flattery; these are counsellors   10
That feelingly persuade me what I am."
Sweet are the uses of adversity,
Which, like the toad, ugly and venomous,
Wears yet a precious jewel in his head;

II.i. 2 *old custom* long familiarity (thus implying that they have been in the forest for some time).   3–4 *these woods . . . court* The perfection of nature as opposed to the evils of court life is a constant theme of European pastoralism. *envious* malicious.   5 *feel we . . . Adam* we are not really troubled or distressed by the punishment of Adam, the severity of seasonal change.   *not* F[1]; THEOBALD, K: "but."   11 *feelingly* (a) through my senses (b) strongly, with persuasion.   12 *uses* benefits, advantages.   13 *toad* References to the venomous toad and to the jewel (toadstone) in its head are multitudinous [K]. It was believed that the more beautiful the stone, the more poisonous the toad.   15 *public haunt* society, the haunts of men.

And this our life, exempt from public haunt,   15
Finds tongues in trees, books in the running brooks,
Sermons in stones, and good in everything.

AMI.   I would not change it. Happy is your Grace
That can translate the stubbornness of fortune
Into so quiet and so sweet a style.   20

DUKE S.   Come, shall we go and kill us venison?
And yet it irks me the poor dappled fools,
Being native burghers of this desert city,
Should, in their own confines, with forked heads
Have their round haunches gor'd.

1. LORD.   Indeed, my lord,   25
The melancholy Jaques grieves at that,
And in that kind swears you do more usurp
Than doth your brother that hath banish'd you.
To-day my Lord of Amiens and myself
Did steal behind him as he lay along   30
Under an oak, whose antique root peeps out
Upon the brook that brawls along this wood;
To the which place a poor sequest'red stag,
That from the hunter's aim had ta'en a hurt,
Did come to languish; and indeed, my lord,   35
The wretched animal heav'd forth such groans
That their discharge did stretch his leathern coat
Almost to bursting, and the big round tears
Cours'd one another down his innocent nose
In piteous chase; and thus the hairy fool,   40
Much marked of the melancholy Jaques,
Stood on th' extremest verge of the swift brook,

---

18 *I would not change it* F¹; DYCE, K add this to the Duke's preceding speech.   19
stubbornness rudeness, rough enmity [K].   22 *irks* displeases. *poor dappled fools*
poor dappled innocents. "Fool" was a term of familiar affection and (especially) of
compassion [K].   23 *desert* uninhabited by man.   24 *with forked heads* A forked
arrow had two prongs, like a pitchfork [K].   27 *kind* respect.   30 *along* stretched
out, at full length.   31 *antique* ancient.   32 *brawls* makes noisy sounds.   33
sequest'red separated from the herd.   38 *tears* Wounded deer were believed actually to weep tears.   39 *Cours'd* pursued.   41 *marked of* observed by.

        Augmenting it with tears.

DUKE S.   But what said Jaques?
        Did he not moralize this spectacle?

1. LORD.   O, yes, into a thousand similes.   45
        First, for his weeping into the needless stream:
        "Poor deer," quoth he, "thou mak'st a testament
        As worldlings do, giving thy sum of more
        To that which had too much." Then, being there alone,
        Left and abandoned of his velvet friends: 50
        " 'Tis right!" quoth he, "thus misery doth part
        The flux of company." Anon a careless herd,
        Full of the pasture, jumps along by him
        And never stays to greet him: "Ay," quoth Jaques,
        "Sweep on, you fat and greasy citizens!   55
        'Tis just the fashion! Wherefore do you look
        Upon that poor and broken bankrupt there?"
        Thus most invectively he pierceth through
        The body of the country, city, court;
        Yea, and of this our life, swearing that we   60
        Are mere usurpers, tyrants, and what's worse,
        To fright the animals and to kill them up
        In their assign'd and native dwelling place.

DUKE S.   And did you leave him in this contemplation?

2. LORD.   We did, my lord, weeping and commenting   65
        Upon the sobbing deer.

DUKE S.   Show me the place.
        I love to cope him in these sullen fits,

---

43 *Augmenting it with tears* Similar hyperbole in the description of grief — and especially of weeping — occurs many times in Shakespeare, from his earliest plays to his latest. Usually it is in serious discourse, but now and then the intent is humorous or satirical. In the present passage the extravagance of the idea is exquisitely appropriate to the half-serious, half-playful tone of the speaker [K]. 44 *moralize this spectacle* take it as the text for a moral discourse; draw moral lessons from it [K].   46 *needless* without need (of more water).   49 *much* F²; F¹: "must." *being there alone* F¹; F², K: "being alone."   50 *velvet* sleek and prosperous; in the "velvet." *friends* ROWE; F¹; "friend," which some editors prefer as referring to his doe rather than to the rest of the herd.   51 *part* depart from, leave.   52 *flux* crowd (literally, flow or confluence). *careless* unconcerned.   57

For then he's full of matter.

1. LORD. I'll bring you to him straight.   *Exeunt.*

◇◇◇◇◇◇◇◇◇◇◇◇◇◇◇

SCENE II.
[*A room in* Duke Frederick's *Palace.*]

Enter Duke [Frederick], *with* Lords.

DUKE.   Can it be possible that no man saw them?
It cannot be. Some villains of my court
Are of consent and sufferance in this.

1. LORD.   I cannot hear of any that did see her.
The ladies her attendants of her chamber   5
Saw her abed, and in the morning early
They found the bed untreasur'd of their mistress.

2. LORD.   My lord, the roynish clown at whom so oft
Your Grace was wont to laugh is also missing.
Hisperia, the princess' gentlewoman,   10
Confesses that she secretly o'erheard
Your daughter and her cousin much commend
The parts and graces of the wrestler
That did but lately foil the sinewy Charles;
And she believes, wherever they are gone,   15
That youth is surely in their company.

DUKE.   Send to his brother, fetch that gallant hither.

---

broken ruined.   58 *invectively* full of bitter denunciation.   59 *of the* F²; F¹: "of."
61 *mere* absolute.   *tyrants* This repeats and intensifies the sense of "usurpers" [K].
what's whatever is.   62 *kill them up* In this use "up" indicates completeness, as
in "drink up," "eat up," "use up" [K].   67 *to cope him* to meet him; to confer
with him [K].   68 *matter* good intellectual stuff; ideas worth listening to [K].
69 *bring* conduct.   *straight* at once.
     II.II. 3 *Are of . . . in this* have connived at this escapade and permitted it [K].
8 *roynish* literally, "scurvy," "mangy" (French "rogneux"), but often used merely
as a term of contempt [K].   13 *parts* good qualities.   *graces* accomplishments.
14 *foil* overcome.   17 *gallant* i.e. Orlando.

If he be absent, bring his brother to me;
I'll make him find him. Do this suddenly,
And let not search and inquisition quail   20
To bring again these foolish runaways.   *Exeunt.*

◇◇◇◇◇◇◇◇◇◇◇◇◇◇◇◇

SCENE III. [*Before* Oliver's *house.*]

Enter Orlando *and* Adam, [*meeting*].

ORL.   Who's there?

ADAM.   What, my young master! O my gentle master!
          O my sweet master! O you memory
          Of old Sir Rowland! Why, what make you here?
          Why are you virtuous? Why do people love you?   5
          And wherefore are you gentle, strong, and valiant?
          Why would you be so fond to overcome
          The bonny prizer of the humorous Duke?
          Your praise is come too swiftly home before you.
          Know you not, master, to some kind of men   10
          Their graces serve them but as enemies?
          No more do yours. Your virtues, gentle master,
          Are sanctified and holy traitors to you.
          O, what a world is this, when what is comely
          Envenoms him that bears it!   15

ORL.   Why, what's the matter?

ADAM.   O unhappy youth,
          Come not within these doors! Within this roof

---

19 *suddenly* at once.   20 *inquisition* inquiry.   *quail* slacken.
  II.III. 3 *memory* personified memory; i.e. one who represents him, in mind and
character, as he lives in my memory [K].   4 *make you* are you doing.   5 *virtuous*
endowed with good qualities of all sorts [K].   7 *fond to* foolish as to.   8 *bonny*
sturdy.   *prizer* professional fighter.   *humorous* full of unpredictable moods.   10
some F²; F¹: "seeme."   11 *graces* good qualities.   12 *No more do yours* your good
qualities serve you no better than theirs serve them [K].   14 *comely* fine, becoming.   15 *Envenoms . . . it* There may be here an implicit allusion to the
poisoned shirt of Nessus by which Hercules was destroyed.   16 *Orl* F²; not in F¹.

The enemy of all your graces lives.
Your brother (no, no brother! yet the son —
Yet not the son — I will not call him son   20
Of him I was about to call his father)
Hath heard your praises, and this night he means
To burn the lodging where you use to lie
And you within it. If he fail of that,
He will have other means to cut you off.   25
I overheard him and his practices.
This is no place, this house is but a butchery.
Abhor it, fear it, do not enter it!

ORL.   Why, whither, Adam, wouldst thou have me go?

ADAM.   No matter whither, so you come not here.   30

ORL.   What, wouldst thou have me go and beg my food,
Or with a base and boist'rous sword enforce
A thievish living on the common road?
This I must do, or know not what to do.
Yet this I will not do, do how I can.   35
I rather will subject me to the malice
Of a diverted blood and bloody brother.

ADAM.   But do not so. I have five hundred crowns,
The thrifty hire I sav'd under your father,
Which I did store to be my foster nurse   40
When service should in my old limbs lie lame
And unregarded age in corners thrown.
Take that, and he that doth the ravens feed,
Yea, providently caters for the sparrow,
Be comfort to my age! Here is the gold;   45
All this I give you. Let me be your servant.

---

23 *use* are accustomed.   26 *practices* plots.   27 *no place* no dwelling place; no fit habitation for you or any man [K].   *butchery* slaughterhouse.   28 *Abhor it* shrink from it — the literal sense [K].   29 *Orl* F²; F¹: "Ad."   37 *a diverted blood* an estranged or alienated kinship. The repetition ("blood" and "bloody," with a change of meaning) is quite in Shakespeare's style [K].   39 *thrifty hire* carefully saved wages [K].   41 *When service . . . lie lame* when my power to do a servant's duty should be paralyzed by the lameness of my old limbs. The ellipsis of the verb in the next line is easily supplied [K].   43–4 *ravens feed . . . sparrow* Cf. JOB XXXVIII, 41; PSALMS, LXXXIV, 3; CXLVII, 9; MATTHEW, X, 29, and LUKE, XII, 6, 24 [K].

Though I look old, yet I am strong and lusty;
For in my youth I never did apply
Hot and rebellious liquors in my blood,
Nor did not with unbashful forehead woo   50
The means of weakness and debility;
Therefore my age is as a lusty winter,
Frosty, but kindly. Let me go with you;
I'll do the service of a younger man
In all your business and necessities.   55

ORL.   O good old man, how well in thee appears
The constant service of the antique world,
When service sweat for duty, not for meed!
Thou art not for the fashion of these times,
Where none will sweat but for promotion,   60
And having that, do choke their service up
Even with the having. It is not so with thee.
But, poor old man, thou prun'st a rotten tree
That cannot so much as a blossom yield
In lieu of all thy pains and husbandry.   65
But come thy ways! We'll go along together,
And ere we have thy youthful wages spent,
We'll light upon some settled low content.

ADAM.   Master, go on, and I will follow thee
To the last gasp with truth and loyalty!   70
From seventeen years till now almost fourscore
Here lived I, but now live here no more.
At seventeen years many their fortunes seek,
But at fourscore it is too late a week;
Yet fortune cannot recompense me better   75
Than to die well and not my master's debtor.   *Exeunt.*

---

47 *lusty* vigorous.   49 *rebellious liquors* i.e. such as attack one's physical consti-
tution [K].   50 *unbashful forehead* impudent and shameless countenance.   57
constant unswerving in fidelity. The repetition of "service" in this and the preceding speech is noteworthy and doubtless intentional [K]. *antique* ancient
(as opposed to the debased world of the present).   58 *meed* reward.   61–2 *do
choke . . . the having* do cease their service as soon as they have earned the reward of advancement.   65 *lieu of* return for.   68 *low content* humble life of
contentment.   71 *seventeen* ROWE; F¹: "seauentie."   74 *too late a week* too late a
time. "Week" is simply used instead of "year" for rhyme and for the sake of

◇◇◇◇◇◇◇◇◇◇◇◇◇◇◇◇◇

SCENE IV.

[*The Forest of Arden. Near a sheepcote.*]

Enter Rosalind *for* Ganymede, Celia *for* Aliena, *and*
Clown, *alias* Touchstone.

ROS.   O Jupiter, how weary are my spirits!

TOUCH.   I care not for my spirits if my legs were not weary.

ROS.   I could find in my heart to disgrace my man's apparel
         and to cry like a woman; but I must comfort the weaker
         vessel, as doublet and hose ought to show itself coura-   5
         geous to petticoat. Therefore, courage, good Aliena!

CEL.   I pray you bear with me; I cannot go no further.

TOUCH.   For my part, I had rather bear with you than bear you.
         Yet I should bear no cross if I did bear you, for I think
         you have no money in your purse.   10

ROS.   Well, this is the Forest of Arden.

TOUCH.   Ay, now am I in Arden, the more fool I! When I was at
         home, I was in a better place; but travellers must be con-
         tent.

                      Enter Corin *and* Silvius.

ROS.   Ay, be so, good Touchstone. — Look you, who comes
         here,   15

---

ironical understatement. Other suggestions are that "a week" is equivalent to "i'
the week" or to "by a week"; but neither is probable [K].
    II.IV. 1 *weary* THEOBALD; F¹: "merry." 4 *comfort* be a support to. 4–5 *weaker
vessel* woman, i.e. Celia. 5 *doublet and hose* close-fitting jacket and breeches.
8 *bear with . . . you* endure you than carry you. Among the most common of
Elizabethan puns. 9 *cross* (a) burden (b) penny — from the Elizabethan coin on
which a cross was stamped. Another of the more common puns of the age. 13–14
be content put up with hardships.

A young man and an old in solemn talk.

COR.   That is the way to make her scorn you still.

SIL.   O Corin, that thou knew'st how I do love her!

COR.   I partly guess; for I have lov'd ere now.

SIL.   No, Corin, being old, thou canst not guess,   20
Though in thy youth thou wast as true a lover
As ever sigh'd upon a midnight pillow.
But if thy love were ever like to mine
(As sure I think did never man love so),
How many actions most ridiculous   25
Hast thou been drawn to by thy fantasy!

COR.   Into a thousand that I have forgotten.

SIL.   O, thou didst then never love so heartily!
If thou rememb'rest not the slightest folly
That ever love did make thee run into,   30
Thou hast not lov'd.
Or if thou has not sat as I do now,
Wearing thy hearer in thy mistress' praise,
Thou hast not lov'd.
Or if thou hast not broke from company   35
Abruptly, as my passion now makes me,
Thou hast not lov'd. O Phebe, Phebe, Phebe!   *Exit.*

ROS.   Alas, poor shepherd! Searching of thy wound,
I have by hard adventure found mine own.

TOUCH.   And I mine. I remember, when I was in love I broke   40
my sword upon a stone and bid him take that for coming a-night to Jane Smile; and I remember the kissing of
her batler, and the cow's dugs that her pretty chopt

---

16 *solemn* serious. Less emphatic than in modern usage [K].   26 *fantasy* fancy,
love.   33 *Wearing* wearying.   36 *passion* Used for any sudden onset of emotion
or strong feeling [K].   38 *Searching of* in probing (a medical metaphor).   *thy
wound* ROWE; F¹: "they would"; F²: "then wound."   39 *hard adventure* an un-
lucky chance [K].   43 *batler* a kind of wooden club used in washing clothes (F¹;
F², K: "batlet").   *chopt* chapped.   45 *peascod* peapod. A rustic lover sometimes
used a curious form of divination. He would tear a peapod so quickly off the vine
as to risk its breaking open, and, if the contents did not fall out, he would give
it to his sweetheart as an auspicious sign of faithful love [K].   45-6 *from whom*

hands had milk'd; and I remember the wooing of a
peascod instead of her, from whom I took two cods, and   45
giving her them again, said with weeping tears, "Wear
these for my sake." We that are true lovers run into
strange capers; but as all is mortal in nature, so is all
nature in love mortal in folly.

ROS.   Thou speak'st wiser than thou art ware of.   50

TOUCH.   Nay, I shall ne'er be ware of mine own wit till I break
my shins against it.

ROS.   Jove, Jove! this shepherd's passion
                 Is much upon my fashion.

TOUCH.   And mine, but it grows something stale with me.   55

CEL.   I pray you, one of you question yond man
If he for gold will give us any food.
I faint almost to death.

TOUCH.   Holla, you clown!

ROS.   Peace, fool! he's not thy kinsman.

COR.   Who calls?

TOUCH.   Your betters, sir.

COR.   Else are they very wretched.   60

ROS.   Peace, I say! — Good even to you, friend.

COR.   And to you, gentle sir, and to you all.

ROS.   I prithee, shepherd, if that love or gold
Can in this desert place buy entertainment,
Bring us where we may rest ourselves and feed.   65

. . . *them again* In saying that he took two peascods from one peascod (referring
probably to the entire plant) and gave them to his mistress, he seems to be quib-
bling on the meaning of "codpiece."   48-9 *as all is mortal . . . folly* as every
living being is subject to death, so every natural man shows his human nature
(his mortality) by foolish actions when he is in love [κ].   50 *ware* aware.   51
ware of on my guard against. *wit* wisdom. Touchstone's remark is ironical. He
knows perfectly well that he is clever, but he pretends that it is always a surprise
to him to discover that he has said something good [κ].   55 *something* somewhat.
61 *you, friend* F²; F¹: "your friend."   64 *desert* uninhabited.

Here's a young maid with travel much oppress'd,
And faints for succour.

COR.   Fair sir, I pity her
And wish, for her sake more than for mine own,
My fortunes were more able to relieve her;
But I am shepherd to another man   70
And do not shear the fleeces that I graze.
My master is of churlish disposition
And little recks to find the way to heaven
By doing deeds of hospitality.
Besides, his cote, his flocks, and bounds of feed   75
Are now on sale, and at our sheepcote now,
By reason of his absence, there is nothing
That you will feed on; but what is, come see,
And in my voice most welcome shall you be.

ROS.   What is he that shall buy his flock and pasture?   80

COR.   That young swain that you saw here but erewhile,
That little cares for buying anything.

ROS.   I pray thee, if it stand with honesty,
Buy thou the cottage, pasture, and the flock,
And thou shalt have to pay for it of us.   85

CEL.   And we will mend thy wages. I like this place
And willingly could waste my time in it.

COR.   Assuredly the thing is to be sold.
Go with me. If you like, upon report,
The soil, the profit, and this kind of life,   90
I will your very faithful feeder be
And buy it with your gold right suddenly.   *Exeunt.*

---

67 *for succour* for lack of help. 72 *churlish* niggardly.   73 *recks* cares (HANMER;
F¹: "wreakes").   75 *cote* cottage. *bounds of feed* pasturage territory [K].   79 *in
my voice* in so far as I have any say in the matter.   81 *erewhile* a little while
ago.   83 *stand* is consistent.   85 *to pay* the money to pay. *of us* from us.   86
mend increase.   87 *waste* spend, pass.   89 *upon report* after receiving further
information.   91 *feeder* servant.   92 *suddenly* promptly.
    II.v. 1 *Ami* CAPELL; not in F¹.   3–4 *turn his . . . throat* adapt his pleasant

◇◇◇◇◇◇◇◇◇◇◇◇◇◇◇◇◇

SCENE V.
[*The Forest. Before* Duke Senior's *cave.*]

Enter Amiens, Jaques, *and others.*

Song.

AMI.
>   Under the greenwood tree
>   Who loves to lie with me,
>   And turn his merry note
>   Unto the sweet bird's throat,
>   Come hither, come hither, come hither!   5
>   Here shall he see
>   No enemy
>   But winter and rough weather.

JAQ.   More, more, I prithee more!

AMI.   It will make you melancholy, Monsieur Jaques.   10

JAQ.   I thank it. More, I prithee more! I can suck melancholy
out of a song as a weasel sucks eggs. More, I prithee
more!

AMI.   My voice is ragged. I know I cannot please you.

JAQ.   I do not desire you to please me; I do desire you to sing.   15
Come, more! another stanzo! Call you 'em stanzos?

AMI.   What you will, Monsieur Jaques.

JAQ.   Nay, I care not for their names; they owe me nothing.
Will you sing?

---

tune to the modulation of the bird's song [K].   5 *hither* Pronounced to rhyme with
"weather."   16 *stanzo* stanza. The word was an elegant one, newly imported from
Italy. Jaques asks whether he prefers this new term to some simple, homespun
word like "verse."   18 *their names* A phantom pun. A borrower was required
to sign an acknowledgment of the loan in the lender's book. Since they owe
Jaques nothing, their names are of no value to him [K].

| AMI. | More at your request than to please myself. | 20 |

JAQ.   Well then, if ever I thank any man, I'll thank you. But
that they call compliment is like th' encounter of two
dog-apes; and when a man thanks me heartily, methinks
I have given him a penny, and he renders me the beggarly thanks. Come, sing! and you that will not, hold   25
your tongues.

AMI.   Well, I'll end the song. Sirs, cover the while; the Duke
will drink under this tree. He hath been all this day to
look you.

JAQ.   And I have been all this day to avoid him. He is too   30
disputable for my company. I think of as many matters
as he; but I give heaven thanks and make no boast of
them. Come, warble, come.

Song.
All together here.

Who doth ambition shun
And loves to live i' th' sun,   35
Seeking the food he eats,
And pleas'd with what he gets,
Come hither, come hither, come hither!
Here shall he see
No enemy   40
But winter and rough weather.

JAQ.   I'll give you a verse to this note that I made yesterday
in despite of my invention.

22 *compliment* ceremony, especially in language [K].   23 *dog-apes* cynocephali —
baboons described as having a head like a dog [K]. When they meet they mock
one another.   24-5 *the beggarly thanks* effusive thanks, such as a beggar returns
for a trifling gift [K].   27 *cover* set the table.   29 *look* look for.   31 *disputable*
inclined to discussion; argumentative [K].   32 *I give heaven thanks* The saying
is founded on a religious scruple. We should remember the fate of Nebuchadnez-
zar, who boasted of his Babylon and gave not God the glory (DANIEL, IV, 28–37;
ACTS, XII, 2–23) [K].   35 *i' th' sun* out in the open air.   42 *note* tune.   43 *in
despite of my invention* to show my imagination what I could do without its aid.
The verses, Jaques implies, are "realistic" rather than imaginative — more truth
than poetry [K].   45 *Thus it goes* F²; F¹ gives the line and the song to Amiens.
Although the present arrangement has been adopted by most modern editors, it
is possible that Jaques hands Amiens a paper and that Amiens, rather than
Jaques, sings the songs.   49 *stubborn* roughly perverse [K].   50 *Ducdame* A

AMI.   And I'll sing it.

JAQ.   Thus it goes: 45

> If it do come to pass
> That any man turn ass,
> Leaving his wealth and ease
> A stubborn will to please,
> Ducdame, ducdame, ducdame!   50
> Here shall he see
> Gross fools as he,
> An if he will come to me.

AMI.   What's that "ducdame"?

JAQ.   'Tis a Greek invocation to call fools into a circle. I'll go   55
        sleep, if I can; if I cannot, I'll rail against all the first-
        born of Egypt.

AMI.   And I'll go seek the Duke. His banquet is prepar'd.

                                         Exeunt [*severally*].

◇◇◇◇◇◇◇◇◇◇◇◇◇◇◇◇◇

SCENE VI. [*The Forest.*]

Enter Orlando *and* Adam.

ADAM.   Dear master, I can go no further. O, I die for food!
        Here lie I down and measure out my grave. Farewell,
        kind master.

---

great puzzle, not yet solved. Amiens does not understand the word and Jaques
quizzically explains it as Greek [K]. There have been countless conjectures, none
satisfactory. The word may be merely meaningless jargon.   55 *Greek* Any un-
intelligible jargon might be called "Greek" in jest [K].   *into a circle* as spirits
were thought to be summoned by spells [K].   56-7 *the first-born of Egypt* all
persons of high degree — since it is the quarrels of such great men that have
banished us from our comforts and forced us to live in the woods. It was the
death of "all the first-born in the land of Egypt" that sent the Israelites forth into
the wilderness. They murmured and looked back longingly at the happy days
when they "sat by the flesh pots [of Egypt], and did eat bread to the full"
(EXODUS, XII, 29-33; XVI, 2-3). These obvious Biblical allusions fit Jaques' dis-
satisfaction with life in the forest. By "the first-born" he may refer to the two
Dukes, whose actions were the cause of his exile from civilized comfort [K].

ORL. Why, how now, Adam? no greater heart in thee? Live
a little, comfort a little, cheer thyself a little. If this un- 5
couth forest yield anything savage, I will either be food
for it or bring it for food to thee. Thy conceit is nearer
death than thy powers. For my sake be comfortable;
hold death awhile at the arm's end. I will here be with
thee presently; and if I bring thee not something to eat, 10
I will give thee leave to die; but if thou diest before I
come, thou art a mocker of my labour. Well said! thou
look'st cheerly, and I'll be with thee quickly. Yet thou
liest in the bleak air. Come, I will bear thee to some
shelter, and thou shalt not die for lack of a dinner if 15
there live anything in this desert. Cheerly, good Adam!

Exeunt.

◇◇◇◇◇◇◇◇◇◇◇◇◇◇◇◇

SCENE VII. *[The Forest. Before the Cave.]*

[A table set out.] Enter Duke Senior, *[Amiens,] and*
Lords, *like* Outlaws.

DUKE S. I think he be transform'd into a beast,
For I can nowhere find him like a man.

1. LORD. My lord, he is but even now gone hence.
Here was he merry, hearing of a song.

DUKE S. If he, compact of jars, grow musical, 5
We shall have shortly discord in the spheres.

II.VI. 5 *comfort* rally thyself.   5–6 *uncouth* wild and uninhabited — literally,
"unknown" [K].   7 *conceit* imagination.   8 *be comfortable* rally thyself [K].   12
Well said well done! Adam has said nothing, but he makes an effort to rally
("Thou look'st cheerly"). This use of "well said" is common [K].   13 *cheerly*
cheerful.

II.VII. 1 *be* The subjunctive in indirect discourse is an Anglo-Saxon construction.
Elizabethan English often keeps it in this particular phrase [K].   2 *like* in the
shape of.   5 *compact of jars* composed of discords.   6 *discord in the spheres* The
spheres of the Ptolemaic astronomy were supposed, in their revolutions about the
earth, to give utterance to a superb harmony, which mortals cannot hear but
which is intelligible to angels and disembodied spirits. For Jaques to become
musical, the Duke thinks, would be as great a contradiction in nature as for the

        Go seek him; tell him I would speak with him.

Enter Jaques.

1. LORD.   He saves my labour by his own approach.

DUKE S.   Why, how now, monsieur! what a life is this,
         That your poor friends must woo your company!   10
         What, you look merrily.

JAQ.   A fool, a fool! I met a fool i' th' forest,
         A motley fool! — a miserable world! —
         As I do live by food, I met a fool,
         Who laid him down and bask'd him in the sun   15
         And rail'd on Lady Fortune in good terms,
         In good set terms — and yet a motley fool.
         "Good morrow, fool," quoth I. "No, sir," quoth he,
         "Call me not fool till heaven hath sent me fortune."
         And then he drew a dial from his poke,   20
         And looking on it with lack-lustre eye,
         Says very wisely, "It is ten o'clock.
         Thus we may see," quoth he, "how the world wags.
         'Tis but an hour ago since it was nine,
         And after one hour more 'twill be eleven;   25
         And so, from hour to hour, we ripe and ripe,
         And then, from hour to hour, we rot and rot;
         And thereby hangs a tale." When I did hear
         The motley fool thus moral on the time,
         My lungs began to crow like chanticleer   30
         That fools should be so deep contemplative;
         And I did laugh sans intermission

---

movement of the heavenly bodies to become discordant [K].   **11** *merrily* cheerful.
Verbs of sensation are regularly followed by adverbs in Elizabethan English [K].
13 *A motley fool* a professional jester — one wearing motley, the parti-coloured
costume worn by such fools.   **17** *In good set terms* in a carefully composed or
"set" speech employing conventional epithets used to rail against Fortune.   **19**
Call . . . fortune The usual proverb is "Fortune favours fools," or, as we say, "A
fool for fortune!" [K].   **20** *a dial from his poke* a sundial from his pocket. Pocket
sundials were often carried by travellers instead of watches [K].   **23** *wags* jogs
along [K].   **28** *thereby hangs a tale* A common expression to introduce an il-
lustrative anecdote [K].   **29** *moral* moralize, speak philosophically.   **30** *crow like
chanticleer* exclaim triumphantly, like the crowing of a cock.   **32** *sans* without.

An hour by his dial. O noble fool!
A worthy fool! Motley 's the only wear!

DUKE S.   What fool is this?   35

JAQ.   O worthy fool! One that hath been a courtier,
And says, if ladies be but young and fair,
They have the gift to know it. And in his brain,
Which is as dry as the remainder biscuit
After a voyage, he hath strange places cramm'd   40
With observation, the which he vents
In mangled forms. O that I were a fool!
I am ambitious for a motley coat.

DUKE S.   Thou shalt have one.

JAQ.   It is my only suit,
Provided that you weed your better judgments   45
Of all opinion that grows rank in them
That I am wise. I must have liberty
Withal, as large a charter as the wind,
To blow on whom I please; for so fools have.
And they that are most galled with my folly,   50
They most must laugh. And why, sir, must they so?
The why is plain as way to parish church:
He that a fool doth very wisely hit
Doth very foolishly, although he smart,
Not to seem senseless of the bob. If not,   55

---

34 *the only wear* the only proper costume; i.e. the fool's is the only proper profession.   39 *dry* Dryness of the brain was thought to cause lack of mental agility and
of inventiveness, but to make the memory strong [K].   *the remainder biscuit* the
leftover remnants of hardtack. "Biscuit" is collective in sense [K].   40 *strange
places* out-of-the-way nooks and corners. Some editors explain "places" as "quo-
tations" or "topics of discourse." This is a recognized Elizabethan meaning, but
does not fit the adjective "strange." Touchstone's store of "observation" consists,
according to Jaques, of commonplaces — bits of trite moralizing — like the speci-
mens given in lines 22–8 [K].   41 *vents* utters.   44 *my only suit* (a) the only re-
quest I have to make (b) the only costume for me.   45 *your better judgments*
your judgment which knows better (than to think me really a fool). If Jaques
is to play the fool, he claims a fool's privileges — one of which is a freedom of
speech that would not be tolerated in a sane man [K].   46 *grows rank* is over-
grown.   48 *Withal* also.   *large* liberal, free from restrictions.   50 *galled with*
irritated by.   55 *Not to seem* THEOBALD; F¹: "Seeme."   *senseless of* insensible to.
bob hit, blow.   55–7 *If not . . . the fool* unless he conceals the fact that he is

    The wise man's folly is anatomiz'd
    Even by the squand'ring glances of the fool.
    Invest me in my motley. Give me leave
    To speak my mind, and I will through and through
    Cleanse the foul body of th' infected world,   60
    If they will patiently receive my medicine.

DUKE S. Fie on thee! I can tell what thou wouldst do.

JAQ. What, for a counter, would I do but good?

DUKE S. Most mischievous foul sin, in chiding sin.
    For thou thyself hast been a libertine,   65
    As sensual as the brutish sting itself;
    And all th' embossed sores and headed evils
    That thou with license of free foot hast caught,
    Wouldst thou disgorge into the general world.

JAQ. Why, who cries out on pride   70
    That can therein tax any private party?
    Doth it not flow as hugely as the sea
    Till that the weary very means do ebb?
    What woman in the city do I name
    When that I say the city woman bears   75
    The cost of princes on unworthy shoulders?
    Who can come in and say that I mean her,
    When such a one as she, such is her neighbour?
    Or what is he of basest function

---

hit by the fool's jest, he acknowledges its applicability, and thus the "squand'ring glances" (the random shots) of the fool have exposed the wise man's folly [K]. *anatomiz'd* revealed as by dissection [K]. *squand'ring* To squander is literally "to scatter about" [K]. *glances* indirect shots.   63 *for a counter* for a token used in computations. Jaques is challenging the Duke to a wager.   66 *brutish sting* carnal lust.   67 *embossed* swollen. *headed* having come to a head (like boils). *evils* diseases. The specific reference appears to be to venereal disease.   68 *license of free foot* unrestrained licentiousness.   70–1 *Why, who . . . private party* what reviler of pride—here used as extravagant display in dress—can blame (tax) an individual (private) person specifically of that sin (since it is common to all humanity)?   73 *Till that . . . do ebb* until the very means of pride (wealth), having become weary (exhausted with overuse) begin to ebb—i.e. the money is used up. *weary* F¹; SINGER, K: "wearer's."   75 *the city woman* The pride and extravagance of Londoners' wives were stock subjects for satire [K].   79 *basest function* lowest occupation in life [K].

That says his bravery is not on my cost,   80
Thinking that I mean him, but therein suits
His folly to the mettle of my speech?
There then! how then? what then? Let me see wherein
My tongue hath wrong'd him. If it do him right,
Then he hath wrong'd himself. If he be free,   85
Why, then my taxing like a wild goose flies,
Unclaim'd of any man. But who comes here?

                    Enter Orlando [*with his sword drawn*].

ORL.   Forbear, and eat no more!

JAQ.   Why, I have eat none yet.

ORL.   Nor shalt not, till necessity be serv'd.

JAQ.   Of what kind should this cock come of?   90

DUKE S.   Art thou thus bolden'd, man, by thy distress,
            Or else a rude despiser of good manners,
            That in civility thou seem'st so empty?

ORL.   You touch'd my vein at first. The thorny point
            Of bare distress hath ta'en from me the show   95
            Of smooth civility; yet am I inland bred
            And know some nurture. But forbear, I say!
            He dies that touches any of this fruit
            Till I and my affairs are answered.

JAQ.   An you will not be answer'd with reason, I must die.   100

DUKE S.   What would you have? Your gentleness shall force
            More than your force move us to gentleness.

ORL.   I almost die for food, and let me have it!

80 *bravery* fine clothes. *is not on my cost* The over-dressed plebeian retorts:
"What business is it of yours? You do not pay for my clothes!" [K].   81–2 *therein
suits . . . speech* by that very retort he shows that the tenour of my speech
applies to his foolish pride [K].   84 *If it do him right* if it does justice to him;
if it applies to him.   85 *he hath wrong'd himself* by resenting my general satire
as if it were personal, he has proved that he is in fault [K].   *free* not guilty.
90 *kind* breed.   93 *civility* good breeding (in general — not in the specific
modern sense of "politeness") [K].   94 *touch'd my vein* hit upon my case, or
(more exactly) my feelings [K].   *at first* at the beginning — when you referred

DUKE S.	Sit down and feed, and welcome to our table.

ORL.   Speak you so gently? Pardon me, I pray you.   105
I thought that all things had been savage here,
And therefore put I on the countenance
Of stern commandment. But whate'er you are
That in this desert inaccessible,
Under the shade of melancholy boughs,   110
Lose and neglect the creeping hours of time —
If ever you have look'd on better days,
If ever been where bells have knoll'd to church,
If ever sat at any good man's feast,
If ever from your eyelids wip'd a tear   115
And know what 'tis to pity and be pitied,
Let gentleness my strong enforcement be;
In the which hope I blush, and hide my sword.

DUKE S.   True is it that we have seen better days,
And have with holy bell been knoll'd to church,   120
And sat at good men's feasts, and wip'd our eyes
Of drops that sacred pity hath engend'red;
And therefore sit you down in gentleness,
And take upon command what help we have
That to your wanting may be minist'red.   125

ORL.   Then but forbear your food a little while,
Whiles, like a doe, I go to find my fawn
And give it food. There is an old poor man
Who after me hath many a weary step
Limp'd in pure love. Till he be first suffic'd,   130
Oppress'd with two weak evils, age and hunger,
I will not touch a bit.

---

to my "distress."   95 *show* appearance.   96 *inland bred* brought up in a settled region — not a rude frontiersman [K].   97 *nurture* good breeding.   99 *answered* provided for. Jaques picks up the word and uses it in its ordinary sense with a pun [K].   100 *An you . . . must die* This flippant comment by Jaques is appropriately put in prose. Various futile attempts to scan it have been made. He puns on "reason" and "raisin," as well as on the two meanings of "answered." The Duke's banquet consisted of fruit and wine [K].   107 *countenance* bearing. 113 *knoll'd* tolled.   117 *enforcement* inducement, means of compelling.   124 *upon command* at your own will.   131 *weak evils* ailments that make one weak [K].

DUKE S.   Go find him out,
And we will nothing waste till you return.

ORL.   I thank ye, and be blest for your good comfort!   [*Exit.*]

DUKE S.   Thou seest we are not all alone unhappy.   135
This wide and universal theatre
Presents more woeful pageants than the scene
Wherein we play in.

JAQ.   All the world's a stage,
And all the men and women merely players.
They have their exits and their entrances,   140
And one man in his time plays many parts,
His acts being seven ages. At first, the infant,
Mewling and puking in the nurse's arms.
Then the whining schoolboy, with his satchel
And shining morning face, creeping like snail   145
Unwillingly to school. And then the lover,
Sighing like furnace, with a woeful ballad
Made to his mistress' eyebrow. Then a soldier,
Full of strange oaths and bearded like the pard,
Jealous in honour, sudden and quick in quarrel,   150
Seeking the bubble reputation
Even in the cannon's mouth. And then the justice,
In fair round belly with good capon lin'd,
With eyes severe and beard of formal cut,
Full of wise saws and modern instances;   155
And so he plays his part. The sixth age shifts
Into the lean and slipper'd pantaloon,

---

133 *waste* consume, eat.   134 *comfort* help.   137 *pageants* theatrical scenes.
138 *All the world's a stage* The comparison of the world to a stage is a common
metaphor in classical, medieval and Renaissance literature. That man's life may
be divided into various "ages," is another ancient idea, although the number of
"ages" has differed with various writers. The number seven, with its mystical
connotations, seems to have originated with Hippocrates and was commonplace
by Shakespeare's time.   143 *Mewling* crying (literally, mewing like a cat).
147 *Sighing like furnace* as a furnace puffs out smoke [K].   149 *strange oaths*
The vocabulary of swearing was much richer and more picturesque in Shakespeare's
time than nowadays [K].   *bearded like the pard* The typical soldier was expected
to wear a full beard and often cultivate long mustaches, which Jaques compares
to those of a panther. Swaggering ruffians imitated the soldier's fashion [K].
150 *Jealous in honour* suspiciously regardful of his honour; sensitive to possible

With spectacles on nose and pouch on side;
His youthful hose, well sav'd, a world too wide
For his shrunk shank, and his big manly voice,   160
Turning again toward childish treble, pipes
And whistles in his sound. Last scene of all,
That ends this strange eventful history,
Is second childishness and mere oblivion,
Sans teeth, sans eyes, sans taste, sans everything.   165

Enter Orlando, *with* Adam.

DUKE S.   Welcome. Set down your venerable burden
            And let him feed.

ORL.   I thank you most for him.

ADAM.   So had you need.
            I scarce can speak to thank you for myself.

DUKE S.   Welcome, fall to. I will not trouble you,   170
            As yet to question you about your fortunes.
            Give us some music; and, good cousin, sing.

Song.

AMI.   Blow, blow, thou winter wind,
               Thou art not so unkind
                  As man's ingratitude.   175
               Thy tooth is not so keen,
               Because thou art not seen,
                  Although thy breath be rude.

---

infractions of it [K].   153 *good capon lin'd* There may be an allusion to the
practice of bribing judges with gifts of capons.   155 *modern instances* trite
examples or illustrations (in proof of his opinions).   157 *pantaloon* old dotard.
Pantalone (like Harlequin) was a stock character in the Italian "commedia dell'
arte." Troupes of Italian dancers and actors often visited England [K].   159 *hose*
breeches.   162 *his* its.   164 *mere* utter, total.   173 *Ami* CAPELL; not in F¹.
174 *unkind* The literal sense of "kind" is "natural," and the Elizabethans seem
always to have been aware of this, even when, as here, the modern meaning is
proper [K].   177 *Because thou art not seen* Dr. Johnson's note is the best: "Thy
rudeness gives the less pain as thou art not seen, as thou art an enemy that dost
not brave us with thy presence, and whose unkindness is therefore not aggravated
by insult" [K].

Heigh-ho, sing heigh-ho, unto the green holly!
Most friendship is feigning, most loving mere folly: 180
    Then, heigh-ho, the holly!
    This life is most jolly.

    Freeze, freeze, thou bitter sky,
    That dost not bite so nigh
        As benefits forgot.   185
    Though thou the waters warp,
    Thy sting is not so sharp
        As friend rememb'red not.
Heigh-ho! sing, &c.

DUKE S. If that you were the good Sir Rowland's son —   190
As you have whisper'd faithfully you were,
And as mine eye doth his effigies witness
Most truly limn'd and living in your face —
Be truly welcome hither. I am the Duke
That lov'd your father. The residue of your fortune,   195
Go to my cave and tell me. Good old man,
Thou art right welcome, as thy master is.
Support him by the arm. Give me your hand,
And let me all your fortunes understand.   *Exeunt.*

---

179 *holly* a traditional symbol of mirth.   180 *feigning* (a) pretense (b) longing,
wishful thinking.   181 *Then* ROWE; F¹: "The."   186 *warp* freeze, turn to ice.
188 *friend rememb'red not* Merely a personal way of expressing the idea of
ingratitude [K].   191 *faithfully* with assurance of your good faith [K].   192
effigies likeness, image.   193 *limn'd* depicted.   197 *Thou* The Duke uses the
respectful "you" to Orlando, the gentleman, but the familiar "thou" to Adam, the
servant [K].   *master* F²; F¹: "masters."

Act Three

◇◇◇

SCENE I. [*A room in the Palace.*]

Enter Duke [Frederick], Lords, *and* Oliver.

DUKE.   Not see him since? Sir, sir, that cannot be!
But were I not the better part made mercy,
I should not seek an absent argument
Of my revenge, thou present. But look to it!
Find out thy brother, wheresoe'er he is;   5
Seek him with candle; bring him dead or living
Within this twelvemonth, or turn thou no more
To seek a living in our territory.
Thy lands, and all things that thou dost call thine
Worth seizure, do we seize into our hands   10
Till thou canst quit thee by thy brother's mouth
Of what we think against thee.

OLI.   O that your Highness knew my heart in this!
I never lov'd my brother in my life.

DUKE.   More villain thou! Well, push him out of doors,   15
And let my officers of such a nature

III.I. 2 *were I . . . made mercy* were I not for the most part composed of mercy. No preposition is omitted. "The better part" is either adverbial accusative or else in a kind of apposition with "I" [K].   3 *argument* subject or object. He means Orlando.   4 *thou present* since you (his brother) are present. 6 *with candle* diligently. Cf. LUKE, XV, 8: "What woman having ten pieces of silver, if she lose one piece, doth not light a candle, and sweep the house, and seek diligently till she find it?"   7 *turn* return.   11 *quit thee . . . mouth* clear thyself by thy brother's testimony [K].   16 *officers of such a nature* those whose business it is to attend to such matters [K].

Make an extent upon his house and lands.
Do this expediently and turn him going.   *Exeunt.*

◇◇◇◇◇◇◇◇◇◇◇◇◇◇◇◇◇

SCENE II. [*The Forest. Near the sheepcote.*]

Enter Orlando, [*with a paper, which he hangs on a tree*].

ORL.   Hang there, my verse, in witness of my love;
          And thou, thrice-crowned Queen of Night, survey
       With thy chaste eye, from thy pale sphere above,
          Thy huntress' name that my full life doth sway.
       O Rosalind! these trees shall be my books,   5
          And in their barks my thoughts I'll character,
       That every eye which in this forest looks
          Shall see thy virtue witness'd everywhere.
       Run, run, Orlando! carve on every tree
       The fair, the chaste, and unexpressive she.   *Exit.* 10

                    Enter Corin *and* [Touchstone the]
                    Clown.

COR.   And how like you this shepherd's life, Master Touch-
       stone?

TOUCH. Truly, shepherd, in respect of itself, it is a good life; but
       in respect that it is a shepherd's life, it is naught. In

17 *Make an extent upon* seize by writ of extent. A writ of extent was a summary
royal process for taking possession of a debtor's estate to satisfy a claim [K].
18 *turn him going* send him packing.
   III.II. 1 *Hang there, my verse* The incident is taken from Lodge's novel. To
hang copies of verses on trees or carve them in the bark is, however, a commonplace of the pastoral genre [K].   2 *thrice-crowned Queen of Night* the moon.
The moon goddess traditionally is conceived of in three forms: Diana on earth,
Cynthia in the sky, and Hecate or Proserpina in the lower world.   3 *pale sphere*
the hollow transparent sphere (concentric with the earth) in which, according
to the Ptolemaic astronomy, the moon is fixed. "Pale" is an epithet transferred
from the moon to the sphere of the moon [K].   4 *Thy huntress' name* Rosalind,
like all young maidens, is one of Diana's nymphs, and Diana is the goddess of
hunting [K].   *sway* rule, control.   6 *character* inscribe.   7 *That* so that.   8 *thy
virtue* thy transcendent excellence in every respect [K].   10 *unexpressive* whose

respect that it is solitary, I like it very well; but in   15
respect that it is private, it is a very vile life. Now in respect it is in the fields, it pleaseth me well; but in respect
it is not in the court, it is tedious. As it is a spare life,
look you, it fits my humour well; but as there is no more
plenty in it, it goes much against my stomach. Hast any   20
philosophy in thee, shepherd?

COR.   No more but that I know the more one sickens, the
worse at ease he is; and that he that wants money,
means, and content is without three good friends; that
the property of rain is to wet and fire to burn; that   25
good pasture makes fat sheep, and that a great cause of
the night is lack of the sun; that he that hath learned
no wit by nature nor art may complain of good breeding, or comes of a very dull kindred.

TOUCH.   Such a one is a natural philosopher. Wast ever in court,   30
shepherd?

COR.   No, truly.

TOUCH.   Then thou art damn'd.

COR.   Nay, I hope.

TOUCH.   Truly thou art damn'd, like an ill-roasted egg, all on   35
one side.

COR.   For not being at court? Your reason.

TOUCH.   Why, if thou never wast at court, thou never saw'st

"virtues" cannot be fully described.   11 *Master* The shepherd addresses Touchstone by the respectful title of "Master" (our "Mr.") and uses the pronoun "you";
whereas Touchstone says, condescendingly, "shepherd," and regularly uses "thou"
[K].   14 *naught* not merely "good for nothing," but in a more positive sense,
"bad," "vile" [K].   16 *private* lonely.   18 *spare* sparing, not luxurious [K].
19 *humour* fancy.   21 *philosophy* This term includes the meaning of what we
now call "science" [K].   28 *wit* knowledge. *complain of* complain of the lack of.
30 *a natural philosopher* Touchstone is really pleased with the clever though
homely answer of the old shepherd, which is, in part, quite in his own vein. He
therefore says, patronizingly: "Such a person, though without education in the
schools, is of a scientific and philosophical turn by nature." There is certainly
no pun on "natural" in the sense of "idiot" [K]. The "profundity" of Corin's
philosophy, however, might suggest the pun.

good manners; if thou never saw'st good manners, then
thy manners must be wicked; and wickedness is sin, and   40
sin is damnation. Thou art in a parlous state, shepherd.

COR.   Not a whit, Touchstone. Those that are good manners
at the court are as ridiculous in the country as the behaviour of the country is most mockable at the court.
You told me you salute not at the court but you kiss   45
your hands. That courtesy would be uncleanly if courtiers were shepherds.

TOUCH.   Instance, briefly. Come, instance.

COR.   Why, we are still handling our ewes, and their fells you
know are greasy.   50

TOUCH.   Why, do not your courtier's hands sweat? and is not the
grease of a mutton as wholesome as the sweat of a man?
Shallow, shallow! A better instance, I say. Come.

COR.   Besides, our hands are hard.

TOUCH.   Your lips will feel them the sooner. Shallow again! A   55
more sounder instance, come.

COR.   And they are often tarr'd over with the surgery of our
sheep, and would you have us kiss tar? The courtier's
hands are perfum'd with civet.

TOUCH.   Most shallow man! Thou worm's meat in respect of a   60
good piece of flesh indeed! Learn of the wise, and perpend. Civet is of a baser birth than tar — the very uncleanly flux of a cat. Mend the instance, shepherd.

---

39 *good manners* The pun which makes Touchstone's burlesque reasoning possible depends on the two meanings of "manners": (a) etiquette, behaviour, and
(b) morals [K].   41 *parlous* perilous.   45 *but you kiss* without kissing.   48 *Instance* proof.   49 *still* always. *fells* fleecy skins.   52 *grease* Perspiration was
believed to be melting body fat. *mutton* sheep.   57 *tarr'd over with the surgery*
as the result of our having acted as surgeons. Tar was used to anoint sore spots,
and the tar-box was a part of the regular equipment of Corin and other shepherds [K].   59 *civet* perfume made from the excrement of the civet cat.
60 *worm's meat* food for worms. A disdainful phrase for "mankind." Here
Touchstone humourously applies it to the shepherd as being a poor kind of man
in comparison with (in respect of) a really excellent specimen of humanity. "Indeed" modifies "good" [K].   61–2 *perpend* attend and consider.   63 *flux* secretion.
Mend the instance improve your demonstration [K].   66 *make incision in thee*
cure thy simple mind by a surgical operation [K].   *raw* uneducated, simple; with

COR.   You have too courtly a wit for me. I'll rest.

TOUCH.   Wilt thou rest damn'd? God help thee, shallow man!   65
          God make incision in thee, thou art raw!

COR.   Sir, I am a true labourer; I earn that I eat, get that I
          wear; owe no man hate, envy no man's happiness; glad
          of other men's good, content with my harm; and the
          greatest of my pride is to see my ewes graze and my   70
          lambs suck.

TOUCH.   That is another simple sin in you: to bring the ewes
          and the rams together and to offer to get your living by
          the copulation of cattle; to be bawd to a bell-wether, and
          to betray a she-lamb of a twelvemonth to a crooked-   75
          pated old cuckoldly ram, out of all reasonable match.
          If thou beest not damn'd for this, the devil himself will
          have no shepherds; I cannot see else how thou shouldst
          scape.

COR.   Here comes young Master Ganymede, my new mistress's   80
          brother.

                    Enter Rosalind, [*reading a paper*].

ROS.   "From the east to western Inde,
                       No jewel is like Rosalinde.
                       Her worth, being mounted on the wind,
                       Through all the world bears Rosalinde.   85
                       All the pictures fairest lin'd
                       Are but black to Rosalinde.

---

a pun on the sense of "sore" or "inflamed" — so as to require the surgeon's treatment [K].   67 *that* what.   68 *owe no man hate* have suffered no wrongs which
call for hatred and vengeance. My account with the world is square [K].
69–70 *the greatest of my pride* Corin mentions a very humble source of satisfaction to prove that he is not guilty of the sin of pride. Touchstone immediately
uses his remark to prove that he is guilty of another deadly sin [K].   72 *simple
sin* foolishly committed sin.   73 *offer* undertake.   76 *cuckoldly* because he
has horns. *out of all reasonable match* quite contrary to any such correspondence
in age and character as befits marriage [K].   77–8 *devil . . . shepherds* The
point is that, if Corin escapes damnation on this score, it will be merely because
shepherds are such objectionable characters that even the devil will not admit
them to his domain; or, perhaps, because the devil has no use for shepherds
since his flock consists altogether of goats (MATTHEW, XXV, 32–41) [K].   79 *scape*
escape.   82 *Inde* the Indies.   86 *lin'd* drawn, delineated.

     Let no face be kept in mind
     But the fair of Rosalinde."

TOUCH. I'll rhyme you so eight years together, dinners and sup- 90
     pers and sleeping hours excepted. It is the right butter-
     women's rank to market.

ROS. Out, fool!

TOUCH. For a taste:

     If a hart do lack a hind,   95
     Let him seek out Rosalinde.
     If the cat will after kind,
     So be sure will Rosalinde.
     Winter garments must be lin'd,
     So must slender Rosalinde.   100
     They that reap must sheaf and bind,
     Then to cart with Rosalinde.
     Sweetest nut hath sourest rind,
     Such a nut is Rosalinde.
     He that sweetest rose will find   105
     Must find love's prick, and Rosalinde.

    This is the very false gallop of verses! Why do you infect
    yourself with them?

ROS. Peace, you dull fool! I found them on a tree.

TOUCH. Truly the tree yields bad fruit.   110

ROS. I'll graff it with you, and then I shall graff it with a
    medlar. Then it will be the earliest fruit i' th' country;

---

89 *the fair* the fairness, the fair face. Not beauty in general, but blonde beauty,
as opposed to "black" [K]. 91-2 *It is the right . . . market* The verses follow
each other jog-trot, exactly like a string of butter-women riding to market [K].
right precise. 97 *after kind* follow its own nature. 99 *Winter* F³; F¹: "Wintred,"
which may be correct as meaning "used in winter." 102 *to cart* Carting was
the regular punishment for Elizabethan whores. 107 *false gallop* canter.
111 *graff* graft. 112 *medlar* a kind of pear, never eaten until it is dead-ripe;
hence the saying that a medlar is not ripe until it is rotten [K]; there is a pun
on the sense of "meddler." *the earliest fruit* With the ordinary medlar — a late
fruit — ripeness and rottenness are coincident; with the kind of meddler this
tree will bear, rottenness will long precede ripeness. Instead of "late medlars,"
we shall have "early meddlers." Rosalind's point is that Touchstone is always

for you'll be rotten ere you be half ripe, and that's the
right virtue of the medlar.

TOUCH.   You have said; but whether wisely or no, let the forest 115
judge.

Enter Celia, *with a writing.*

ROS.   Peace!
Here comes my sister reading. Stand aside.

CEL.   "Why should this a desert be,
                  For it is unpeopled? No!   120
              Tongues I'll hang on every tree
                  That shall civil sayings show:
              Some, how brief the life of man
                  Runs his erring pilgrimage,
              That the stretching of a span   125
                  Buckles in his sum of age;
              Some, of violated vows
                  'Twixt the souls of friend and friend;
              But upon the fairest boughs,
                  Or at every sentence end,   130
              Will I 'Rosalinda' write,
                  Teaching all that read to know
              The quintessence of every sprite
                  Heaven would in little show.
              Therefore heaven Nature charg'd   135
                  That one body should be fill'd
              With all graces wide-enlarg'd.
                  Nature presently distill'd

in a hurry to talk impertinent nonsense [K].   114 *right* true.   119 *a desert*
ROWE; F¹: "desert."   122 *civil* civilized (such as one might not ordinarily find
in a "desert" place).   124 *erring* wandering.   125 *That* so that. *span* the
distance from the end of the thumb to the end of the little finger when both
are extended or held in a circle [K].   126 *Buckles in* encompasses.   133-4 *The
quintessence . . . show* that heaven wished to exhibit in miniature (in one individual) the finest essential quality of every nature [K]. The idea of the individual
as a small model (or microcosm) of the larger universe is a medieval commonplace. The "quintessence" in medieval philosophy was the "soul of the world,"
an element transcending the other four and of greater purity. *sprite* spirit.
137 *wide-enlarg'd* in their fullest manifestation [K].   138 *presently* forthwith.

> Helen's cheek, but not her heart,
> > Cleopatra's majesty,   140
> Atalanta's better part,
> > Sad Lucretia's modesty.
> Thus Rosalinde of many parts
> > By heavenly synod was devis'd,
> Of many faces, eyes, and hearts,   145
> > To have the touches dearest priz'd.
> Heaven would that she these gifts should have,
> And I to live and die her slave."

ROS.   O most gentle pulpiter! what tedious homily of love have you wearied your parishioners withal, and never 150 cried, "Have patience, good people"!

CEL.   How now? Back, friends. Shepherd, go off a little. Go with him, sirrah.

TOUCH.   Come, shepherd, let us make an honourable retreat; though not with bag and baggage, yet with scrip and 155 scrippage.

Exeunt [Corin *and* Touchstone].

CEL.   Didst thou hear these verses?

ROS.   O, yes, I heard them all, and more too; for some of them had in them more feet than the verses would bear.

CEL.   That's no matter. The feet might bear the verses.   160

ROS.   Ay, but the feet were lame, and could not bear themselves without the verse, and therefore stood lamely in the verse.

---

139 *her heart* for that was inconstant (ROWE; F¹: "his heart")   141 *better part* chief good quality. Since Atalanta was most famous as a runner (cf. line 264), her fine figure and physical alertness of bearing may be meant [K].   146 *touches* traits.   149 *pulpiter* preacher (SPEDDING; F¹: "Jupiter"). Spedding's emendation is irresistible [K]. Although widely accepted, it is difficult to justify on any textual grounds, however.   152 *Back, friends* Addressed to Corin and Touchstone [K].   155–6 *scrip and scrippage* wallet or pouch and its contents. Touchstone adapts the stock phrase ("bag and baggage") to fit their light accoutrements [K]. 159 *bear* allow. In the next line Celia puns on "bear" in the sense of "carry." Rosalind replies that the feet were so lame that they could not carry themselves out of the verse and had to stay in it in their lameness [K].   165 *should be* came to be.   166 *nine days* A "nine days' wonder" is a common expression,

CEL.   But didst thou hear without wondering how thy name
should be hang'd and carved upon these trees?   165

ROS.   I was seven of the nine days out of the wonder before
you came; for look here what I found on a palm tree.
I was never so berhym'd since Pythagoras' time that I
was an Irish rat, which I can hardly remember.

CEL.   Trow you who hath done this?   170

ROS.   Is it a man?

CEL.   And a chain that you once wore, about his neck. Change
you colour?

ROS.   I prithee who?

CEL.   O Lord, Lord! it is a hard matter for friends to meet; 175
but mountains may be remov'd with earthquakes, and
so encounter.

ROS.   Nay, but who is it?

CEL.   Is it possible?

ROS.   Nay, I prithee now with most petitionary vehemence,   180
tell me who it is.

CEL.   O wonderful, wonderful, and most wonderful wonderful! and yet again wonderful, and after that, out of all
hooping!

ROS.   Good my complexion! Dost thou think, though I am   185
caparison'd like a man, I have a doublet and hose in

---

still current.   168 *Pythagoras' time* A reference to the Pythagorean doctrine of
the transmigration of souls [K].   *that* when.   169 *an Irish rat* The Irish sor-
cerers could kill rats and other animals, even men, by means of rhymed spells
is an old belief [K].   170 *Trow you who* who do you think.   175–6 *friends . . .
mountains* An allusion to the old proverb: "Friends may meet, but mountains
never greet."   176 *remov'd with* moved by.   177 *encounter* be brought together.
183–4 *out of all hooping* beyond every possibility of whooping to express [K].
185 *Good my complexion* The Lord have mercy on my woman's nature! "Complexion" often means "temperament," and this sense accords with "disposition"
(line 187). There is no allusion to blushing: Rosalind's whole speech is concerned,
not with feminine modesty, but with impatient curiosity [K].   186 *caparison'd* be-
decked (a term usually applied to horses).

my disposition? One inch of delay more is a South Sea
of discovery. I prithee tell me who is it quickly, and
speak apace. I would thou couldst stammer, that thou
mightst pour this conceal'd man out of thy mouth as 190
wine comes out of a narrow-mouth'd bottle — either too
much at once, or none at all. I prithee take the cork out
of thy mouth, that I may drink thy tidings.

CEL.   So you may put a man in your belly.

ROS.   Is he of God's making? What manner of man? Is his 195
head worth a hat? or his chin worth a beard?

CEL.   Nay, he hath but a little beard.

ROS.   Why, God will send' more, if the man will be thankful!
Let me stay the growth of his beard, if thou delay me
not the knowledge of his chin.   200

CEL.   It is young Orlando, that tripp'd up the wrestler's heels
and your heart both in an instant.

ROS.   Nay, but the devil take mocking! Speak sad brow and
true maid.

CEL.   I' faith, coz, 'tis he.   205

ROS.   Orlando?

CEL.   Orlando.

ROS.   Alas the day! what shall I do with my doublet and hose?
What did he when thou saw'st him? What said he? How
look'd he? Wherein went he? What makes he here? Did 210
he ask for me? Where remains he? How parted he with

187-8 *One inch . . . discovery* another inch of delay will seem to me as long
as the time needed for a voyage that would explore the whole South Pacific [K].
195 *of God's making* Merely a proverbial phrase for a normal human creature [K].
199 *stay* wait for.   203-4 *sad brow and true maid* seriously and truly (upon your
honour).   210 *Wherein went he* how was he dressed? *What makes he* what is
he doing?   214 *Gargantua's mouth* Gargantua is the giant in Rabelais who
swallows five pilgrims and their staves in a salad. But, independently of Rabelais,
Gargantua was a popular figure in England before 1572, and a "historie of
Gargantua" was entered in the Stationers' Register in 1594 [K].   215-17 *To say
ay . . . catechism* to give even the briefest possible answers to these questions
would be more than to go through an entire catechism.   219 *freshly* vigorous.

thee? and when shalt thou see him again? Answer me
in one word.

CEL.   You must borrow me Gargantua's mouth first; 'tis a
word too great for any mouth of this age's size. To say   215
ay and no to these particulars is more than to answer
in a catechism.

ROS.   But doth he know that I am in this forest, and in man's
apparel? Looks he as freshly as he did the day he
wrestled?   220

CEL.   It is as easy to count atomies as to resolve the propositions of a lover; but take a taste of my finding him, and
relish it with good observance. I found him under a
tree, like a dropp'd acorn.

ROS.   It may well be called Jove's tree when it drops such   225
fruit.

CEL.   Give me audience, good madam.

ROS.   Proceed.

CEL.   There lay he stretch'd along like a wounded knight.

ROS.   Though it be pity to see such a sight, it well becomes   230
the ground.

CEL.   Cry "holla" to thy tongue, I prithee. It curvets unseason-
ably. He was furnish'd like a hunter.

ROS.   O, ominous! he comes to kill my heart.

CEL.   I would sing my song without a burden. Thou bring'st   235
me out of tune.

---

221 *atomies* specks in a sunbeam.   *resolve the propositions* answer the questions.
222 *take a taste . . . him* accept a sample (of the information you ask for), con-
sisting in (an account of) how I found him [K].   225 *Jove's tree* The oak was con-
sidered sacred to Jove.   *drops such* F²; F¹: "drops forth"; K: "drops forth such."
229 *along* at full length.   231 *the ground* Sometimes explained as "the background of the picture." Apparently, however, Rosalind means merely that the
earth on which Orlando lies is adorned by his beauty. She is humorously con-
scious of her own sentimentality [K].   232 *to thy* ROWE; F¹: "to the."   233 *furnish'd* accoutred.   234 *heart* ROWE; F¹: "Hart," which indicates the pun.   235 *burden* refrain.

ROS.   Do you not know I am a woman? When I think, I must
       speak. Sweet, say on.

CEL.   You bring me out.

                Enter Orlando *and* Jaques.

       Soft! comes he not here?   240

ROS.   'Tis he! Slink by, and note him.   [*They step aside.*]

JAQ.   I thank you for your company; but, good faith, I had
       as lief have been myself alone.

ORL.   And so had I; but yet for fashion sake I thank you too
       for your society.   245

JAQ.   God buy you! Let's meet as little as we can.

ORL.   I do desire we may be better strangers.

JAQ.   I pray you mar no more trees with writing love songs
       in their barks.

ORL.   I pray you mar no moe of my verses with reading them   250
       ill-favouredly.

JAQ.   Rosalind is your love's name?

ORL.   Yes, just.

JAQ.   I do not like her name.

ORL.   There was no thought of pleasing you when she was   255
       christen'd.

JAQ.   What stature is she of?

ORL.   Just as high as my heart.

JAQ.   You are full of pretty answers. Have you not been
       acquainted with goldsmiths' wives, and conn'd them out 260
       of rings?

---

237 *a woman* Cf. lines 185–7. Rosalind's femininity is emphasized in this part of
the scene. Note the change when Orlando enters and she begins to act a young
man's part [K].   239 *bring me out* confuse me.   241 *by* aside.   242–3 *had as
lief* would as gladly.   246 *God buy you* God be with you and God save you — a
common Elizabethan form (F¹; K: "God b' wi' you").   250 *moe* more.   251 *ill-
favouredly* unhandsomely — literally, in an ugly fashion [K].   253 *just* exactly,
just so.   260–1 *conn'd them out of rings* your replies are as pretty, and as trite,

| ORL. | Not so; but I answer you right painted cloth, from whence you have studied your questions. |

JAQ.   You have a nimble wit; I think 'twas made of Atalanta's heels. Will you sit down with me? and we two will rail 265 against our mistress the world and all our misery.

ORL.   I will chide no breather in the world but myself, against whom I know most faults.

JAQ.   The worst fault you have is to be in love.

ORL.   'Tis a fault I will not change for your best virtue. I am 270 weary of you.

JAQ.   By my troth, I was seeking for a fool when I found you.

ORL.   He is drown'd in the brook. Look but in and you shall see him.

JAQ.   There I shall see mine own figure.   275

ORL.   Which I take to be either a fool or a cipher.

JAQ.   I'll tarry no longer with you. Farewell, good Signior Love.

ORL.   I am glad of your departure. Adieu, good Monsieur Melancholy.   280

[*Exit* Jaques. Celia *and* Rosalind *come forward.*]

ROS.   [*aside to* Celia] I will speak to him like a saucy lackey, and under that habit play the knave with him. — Do you hear, forester?

ORL.   Very well. What would you?

ROS.   I pray you, what is't o'clock?   285

---

as if you had learned by heart a lot of the posies (i.e. poesics) engraved on rings [K].   262 *right* regular.   *painted cloth* Orlando retorts that his answers are no less original than Jaques's questions. Painted or stained cloth was a cheaper substitute for arras (tapestry hangings). The pictures and mottoes were painted in oil or stained in water colours instead of being woven into the fabric [K]. 267 *breather* living creature.   276 *cipher* A common pun on "figure."   282 *under that habit* in that role.

ORL.   You should ask me, what time o' day. There's no clock
in the forest.

ROS.   Then there is no true lover in the forest; else sighing
every minute and groaning every hour would detect the
lazy foot of Time as well as a clock.   290

ORL.   And why not the swift foot of Time? Had not that been
as proper?

ROS.   By no means, sir. Time travels in divers paces with divers
persons. I'll tell you who Time ambles withal, who Time
trots withal, who Time gallops withal, and who he 295
stands still withal.

ORL.   I prithee, who doth he trot withal?

ROS.   Marry, he trots hard with a young maid between the
contract of her marriage and the day it is solemniz'd.
If the interim be but a se'nnight, Time's pace is so hard 300
that it seems the length of seven year.

ORL.   Who ambles Time withal?

ROS.   With a priest that lacks Latin and a rich man that hath
not the gout; for the one sleeps easily because he cannot
study, and the other lives merrily because he feels no 305
pain; the one lacking the burden of lean and wasteful
learning, the other knowing no burden of heavy tedious
penury. These Time ambles withal.

ORL.   Who doth he gallop withal?

ROS.   With a thief to the gallows; for though he go as softly 310
as foot can fall, he thinks himself too soon there.

ORL.   Who stays it still withal?

ROS.   With lawyers in the vacation; for they sleep between
term and term, and then they perceive not how time
moves.   315

289-90 *detect the lazy foot* show the tardy progress [K].   294 *withal* with.
298 *trots hard* trots with a slow uneven pace.   300 *se'nnight* week.   306 *wasteful*
wasting (in an active sense) [K].   310 *softly* slowly.   320 *cony* rabbit. *kindled*
born. The word is restricted to hares and rabbits [K].   321 *purchase* acquire.
322 *removed* remote.   323 *religious* belonging to a religious order — perhaps a
hermit [K].   325 *inland man* city dweller. *courtship* the life and manners of

ORL.   Where dwell you, pretty youth?

ROS.   With this shepherdess, my sister; here in the skirts of the
forest, like fringe upon a petticoat.

ORL.   Are you native of this place?

ROS.   As the cony that you see dwell where she is kindled.   320

ORL.   Your accent is something finer than you could purchase
in so removed a dwelling.

ROS.   I have been told so of many. But indeed an old religious
uncle of mine taught me to speak, who was in his youth
an inland man; one that knew courtship too well, for   325
there he fell in love. I have heard him read many lec-
tures against it; and I thank God I am not a woman,
to be touch'd with so many giddy offences as he hath
generally tax'd their whole sex withal.

ORL.   Can you remember any of the principal evils that he   330
laid to the charge of women?

ROS.   There were none principal. They were all like one another as halfpence are, every one fault seeming mon-
strous till his fellow-fault came to match it.

ORL.   I prithee recount some of them.   335

ROS.   No, I will not cast away my physic but on those that are
sick. There is a man haunts the forest that abuses our
young plants with carving "Rosalind" on their barks;
hangs odes upon hawthorns, and elegies on brambles;
all, forsooth, deifying the name of Rosalind. If I could   340
meet that fancy-monger, I would give him some good
counsel, for he seems to have the quotidian of love upon
him.

ORL.   I am he that is so love-shak'd. I pray you tell me your
remedy.   345

---

the court — with an obvious pun [K].   328 *touch'd* tainted. *giddy offences* faults
due to instability of character [K].   329 *generally* universally, without exception.
340 *deifying* F²; F¹: "defying."   341 *fancy-monger* dealer in fancy — a common
Elizabethan term for "love."   342 *quotidian* an ague whose attacks come every
day [K].   344 *love-shak'd* suffering from the fever of love.

ROS.   There is none of my uncle's marks upon you. He taught
        me how to know a man in love; in which cage of rushes
        I am sure you are not prisoner.

ORL.   What were his marks?

ROS.   A lean cheek, which you have not; a blue eye and 350
        sunken, which you have not; an unquestionable spirit,
        which you have not; a beard neglected, which you have
        not. But I pardon you for that, for simply your having
        in beard is a younger brother's revenue. Then your hose
        should be ungarter'd, your bonnet unbanded, your sleeve 355
        unbutton'd, your shoe untied, and everything about you
        demonstrating a careless desolation. But you are no such
        man: you are rather point-device in your accoustrements,
        as loving yourself, than seeming the lover of any other.

ORL.   Fair youth, I would I could make thee believe I love.   360

ROS.   Me believe it? You may as soon make her that you love
        believe it, which I warrant she is apter to do than to
        confess she does. That is one of the points in the which
        women still give the lie to their consciences. But in good
        sooth, are you he that hangs the verses on the trees 365
        wherein Rosalind is so admired?

ORL.   I swear to thee, youth, by the white hand of Rosalind,
        I am that he, that unfortunate he.

ROS.   But are you so much in love as your rhymes speak?

ORL.   Neither rhyme nor reason can express how much.   370

ROS.   Love is merely a madness, and, I tell you, deserves as
        well a dark house and a whip as madmen do; and the

---

347 *cage of rushes* a kind of prison from which any but a willing captive may
easily escape. "Cage" was the regular word for a local lockup [K].   348 *are not* F²;
F¹: "art not."   350 *blue eye* eye with dark circles under it [K].   351 *unquestion-
able* unwilling to engage in conversation.   353 *simply* to tell the simple truth.
353-4 *having in beard* assets in the way of beard [K].   354 *younger brother's
revenue* The allowance granted a younger bother was proverbially small.
354-7 *your hose ungarter'd . . . careless desolation* Such details of neglect of
one's personal appearance, as indicating preoccupation of mind, were recognized
as conventional marks of a lover [K].   355 *unbanded* Hatbands were sometimes
very elaborate. They were removable, and were frequently changed [K].   357 *a
careless desolation* an utterly dispirited condition without care for one's appearance.   358 *point-device* carefully attended to; spick and span. Not equivalent,

reason why they are no so punish'd and cured is that
the lunacy is so ordinary that the whippers are in love
too. Yet I profess curing it by counsel.   375

ORL.   Did you ever cure any so?

ROS.   Yes, one, and in this manner. He was to imagine me his
love, his mistress; and I set him every day to woo me.
At which time would I, being but a moonish youth,
grieve, be effeminate, changeable, longing, and liking, 380
proud, fantastical, apish, shallow, inconstant, full of
tears, full of smiles; for every passion something and for
no passion truly anything, as boys and women are for
the most part cattle of this colour; would now like him,
now loathe him; then entertain him, then forswear him; 385
now weep for him, then spit at him; that I drave my
suitor from his mad humour of love to a living humour
of madness, which was, to forswear the full stream of the
world and to live in a nook merely monastic. And thus
I cur'd him; and this way will I take upon me to wash 390
your liver as clean as a sound sheep's heart, that there
shall not be one spot of love in't.

ORL.   I would not be cured, youth.

ROS.   I would cure you, if you would but call me Rosalind
and come every day to my cote and woo me.   395

ORL.   Now, by the faith of my love, I will! Tell me where it is.

ROS.   Go with me to it, and I'll show it you; and by the way
you shall tell me where in the forest you live. Will you
go?

---

however, to "affectedly nice" [K]. *accoustrements* accoutrements, outfit.   364 *still*
always.   364-5 *good sooth* honest truth.   372 *a dark house and a whip* the usual
expert treatment of lunatics in old times [K].   375 *profess curing* know how to
cure.   379 *moonish* fickle, changeable like the moon.   380 *liking* affectionate.
381 *fantastical* ruled by the fancy of the moment. *apish* whimsical. *shallow*
frivolous.   382 *passion* emotion.   384 *colour* kind, sort.   385 *entertain him* welcome him. *forswear him* flatly refuse to have anything to do with him; solemnly
renounce his acquaintance [K].   386 *that* so that.   387-8 *from his mad . . . madness* from his crazy whim of being in love to an actual condition of madness [K].
389 *merely monastic* exactly like a monk.   391 *liver* Supposed to be the seat of
the passion of love [K].   395 *cote* cottage.

ORL.   With all my heart, good youth.   400

ROS.   Nay, you must call me Rosalind. Come, sister, will you
          go?   *Exeunt.*

◇◇◇◇◇◇◇◇◇◇◇◇◇◇◇◇◇

SCENE III. [*The Forest. Near the sheepcote.*]

Enter [Touchstone the] Clown, Audrey; *and* Jaques
    [*behind*].

TOUCH.   Come apace, good Audrey. I will fetch up your goats,
          Audrey. And how, Audrey, am I the man yet? Doth my
          simple feature content you?

AUD.   Your features? Lord warrant us! What features?

TOUCH.   I am here with thee and thy goats, as the most capricious   5
          poet, honest Ovid, was among the Goths.

JAQ.   [*aside*] O knowledge ill-inhabited, worse than Jove in a
          thatch'd house!

TOUCH.   When a man's verses cannot be understood, nor a man's
          good wit seconded with the forward child, understand-   10
          ing, it strikes a man more dead than a great reckoning
          in a little room. Truly, I would the gods had made thee
          poetical.

III.III. 1 *Audrey* A shortened form of "Etheldreda" [K].   3 *simple feature*
general appearance.   4 *features* Audrey apparently takes the word in the sense
of "bodily parts." The nature of the joke, however, is not clear and has been
much debated.   5 *capricious* sportive; with a suggestion also of Ovid's elegant
tricks of style or conceits. There is an obvious pun on the Latin "caper," "goat,"
from which "capricious" was thought to be derived [K].   6 *honest Ovid* . . .
Goths Ovid was banished by the Emperor Augustus to live among the Getae,
formerly identified with the Goths. As the author of the ARS AMATORIA, supposedly
the cause of his banishment, Ovid could hardly be called an "honest" (meaning
"chaste") poet.   7 *ill-inhabited* poorly lodged.   7–8 *Jove . . . house* Ovid in
METAMORPHOSES, VIII, tells of the visit of Jove and Mercury in disguise to the

AUD.	I do not know what poetical is. Is it honest in deed and word? Is it a true thing?

15

TOUCH.	No, truly; for the truest poetry is the most feigning, and lovers are given to poetry; and what they swear in poetry may be said, as lovers, they do feign.

AUD.	Do you wish then that the gods had made me poetical?

TOUCH.	I do truly. For thou swear'st to me thou art honest. Now if thou wert a poet, I might have some hope thou didst feign.

20

AUD.	Would you not have me honest?

TOUCH.	No, truly, unless thou wert hard-favour'd; for honesty coupled to beauty is to have honey a sauce to sugar.

25

JAQ.	[aside] A material fool!

AUD.	Well, I am not fair; and therefore I pray the gods make me honest.

TOUCH.	Truly, and to cast away honesty upon a foul slut were to put good meat into an unclean dish.

30

AUD.	I am not a slut, though I thank the gods I am foul.

TOUCH.	Well, praised be the gods for thy foulness! Sluttishness may come hereafter. But be it as it may be, I will marry thee; and to that end I have been with Sir Oliver Martext, the vicar of the next village, who hath promis'd to meet me in this place of the forest and to couple us.

35

JAQ.	[aside] I would fain see this meeting.

AUD.	Well, the gods give us joy!

humble cottage of Baucis and Philemon.   9 *a man's verses* As the Goths could not understand Ovid's verses, so Audrey and her goats cannot understand Touch-stone's "good wit." There is no suggestion that the clown has been wooing her in verse [K].   11–12 *great reckoning . . . little room* a huge bill for meat and drink in an inn where the accommodation is scanty [K]. Some have suspected an allusion to the death of Marlowe in a Deptford tavern in 1593; he had quarrelled over the reckoning with his murderer, Ingram Frizer.   17–18 *what they swear . . . do feign* what they swear as poets, it may be said that they feign as lovers, for their versified protestations are merely lovers' perjuries [K].   20 *honest* chaste.   24 *hard-favour'd* ugly.   26 *material* full of ideas.   34 *Sir* A priest's title ("dominus") [K].

TOUCH.   Amen. A man may, if he were of a fearful heart, stagger
in this attempt; for here we have no temple but the   40
wood, no assembly but horn-beasts. But what though?
Courage! As horns are odious, they are necessary. It is
said, "Many a man knows no end of his goods." Right!
Many a man has good horns and knows no end of them.
Well, that is the dowry of his wife; 'tis none of his own   45
getting. Horns? Even so. Poor men alone? No, no! the
noblest deer hath them as huge as the rascal. Is the
single man therefore blessed? No; as a wall'd town is
more worthier than a village, so is the forehead of a
married man more honourable than the bare brow of a   50
bachelor; and by how much defence is better than no
skill, by so much is a horn more precious than to want.

Enter Sir Oliver Martext.

Here comes Sir Oliver. Sir Oliver Martext, you are well
met. Will you dispatch us here under this tree, or shall
we go with you to your chapel?   55

OLI.   Is there none here to give the woman?

TOUCH.   I will not take her on gift of any man.

OLI.   Truly, she must be given, or the marriage is not lawful.

JAQ.   [*comes forward*] Proceed, proceed! I'll give her.

TOUCH.   Good even, good Master What-ye-call't. How do you,   60
sir? You are very well met. Goddild you for your last
company. I am very glad to see you. Even a toy in hand
here, sir. Nay, pray be cover'd.

JAQ.   Will you be married, motley?

---

41 *horn-beasts* The unfailing jest on the horns of a cuckold [K].   42 *necessary*
inevitable.   43 *Many a man . . . goods* many a man does not realize that his
wealth is not boundless [K].   44 *knows no end of them* does not perceive their
points sprouting from his forehead [K].   47 *rascal* a deer that is lean and out
of condition [K].   51 *defence* skill in fencing.   52 *to want* to lack (horns).
54 *dispatch us* finish our business — marry us [K].   57 *on gift of any man* with
the implication that the giver has already used her.   58 *she must be given* the
formula of giving in marriage must be carried out [K].   61 *Goddild you* God
yield (i.e. pay, reward) you. A common colloquial contraction [K].   62 *a toy in
hand* a small piece of work underway [K].   63 *be cover'd* don't take off your hat.

TOUCH.   As the ox hath his bow, sir, the horse his curb, and the   65
          falcon her bells, so man hath his desires; and as pigeons
          bill, so wedlock would be nibbling.

JAQ.   And will you, being a man of your breeding, be married
          under a bush like a beggar? Get you to church, and have
          a good priest that can tell you what marriage is. This   70
          fellow will but join you together as they join wainscot;
          then one of you will prove a shrunk panel, and like
          green timber warp, warp.

TOUCH.   [aside] I am not in the mind, but I were better to be
          married of him than of another; for he is not like to   75
          marry me well; and not being well married, it will be
          a good excuse for me hereafter to leave my wife.

JAQ.   Go thou with me and let me counsel thee.

TOUCH.   Come, sweet Audrey.
          We must be married, or we must live in bawdry.   80
          Farewell, good Master Oliver: not

                    O sweet Oliver,
                    O brave Oliver,
                 Leave me not behind thee!

          but   85

                    Wind away,
                    Be gone, I say!
                 I will not to wedding with thee.

                        [Exeunt Jaques, Touchstone, and Au-
                        drey.]

---

65 *bow* the rounded collar that forms part of the yoke [K].   66 *her* "Falcon"
is feminine; the male bird is called "tercel" or "tassel" [K].   *bells* regularly
attached to falcons.   70 *a good priest* Jaques does not imply that Sir Oliver
is not in orders. He means that, being an uneducated hedge-priest, he will not
expound the duties of marriage adequately. Lacking such instruction, the wedded
pair will not live happily and one or the other of them will "warp" — become
estranged or unfaithful. Touchstone (punning even in soliloquy) chooses to take
"well" in the sense of "legally" [K].   79 *Touch* F²: "Clown"; F¹: "Ol."   80 *bawdry*
immorality.   82–8 *O sweet Oliver . . . with thee* Printed as prose in F¹, the lines
are actually snatches from a popular ballad of the time.

| OLI. | 'Tis no matter. Ne'er a fantastical knave of them all shall flout me out of my calling.   *Exit.* 90 |

◇◇◇◇◇◇◇◇◇◇◇◇◇◇◇◇

SCENE IV. [*The Forest. Near the sheepcote.*]

Enter Rosalind *and* Celia.

ROS. Never talk to me! I will weep.

CEL. Do, I prithee; but yet have the grace to consider that tears do not become a man.

ROS. But have I not cause to weep?

CEL. As good cause as one would desire. Therefore weep. 5

ROS. His very hair is of the dissembling colour.

CEL. Something browner than Judas's. Marry, his kisses are Judas's own children.

ROS. I' faith, his hair is of a good colour.

CEL. An excellent colour. Your chestnut was ever the only 10 colour.

ROS. And his kissing is as full of sanctity as the touch of holy bread.

90 *flout me out of my calling* make me give up my profession by his jeers. The honours remain with Sir Oliver, who, though perhaps not highly educated, is certainly in orders and scrupulous about the marriage ceremony (line 58) [K].

III.IV. 6 *the dissembling colour* red, like the hair and beard of Judas. The tradition that Judas had red hair goes back a long way and has lasted until modern times. Hence red-haired men were regarded as untrustworthy [K]. 8 *Judas's own children* instruments of betrayal. The "Judas kiss" was proverbial. 10–11 *the only colour* the best of all colours.   13 *holy bread* bread brought to church to be blessed by the priest and distributed among the congregation. It should not be confused with the bread consecrated in the mass [K].   14 *cast* (a) cast off, discarded (b) cold marble — since Diana was a common subject for

| CEL. | He hath bought a pair of cast lips of Diana. A nun of winter's sisterhood kisses not more religiously; the very ice of chastity is in them. | 15 |

ROS.   But why did he swear he would come this morning, and comes not?

CEL.   Nay, certainly there is no truth in him.

ROS.   Do you think so?   20

CEL.   Yes. I think he is not a pickpurse nor a horse-stealer; but for his verity in love, I do think him as concave as a covered goblet or a worm-eaten nut.

ROS.   Not true in love?

CEL.   Yes, when he is in; but I think he is not in.   25

ROS.   You have heard him swear downright he was.

CEL.   "Was" is not "is." Besides, the oath of a lover is no stronger than the word of a tapster: they are both the confirmer of false reckonings. He attends here in the forest on the Duke your father.   30

ROS.   I met the Duke yesterday and had much question with him. He ask'd me of what parentage I was. I told him, of as good as he. So he laugh'd and let me go. But what talk we of fathers when there is such a man as Orlando?

CEL.   O, that's a brave man! He writes brave verses, speaks 35 brave words, swears brave oaths, and breaks them bravely — quite traverse, athwart the heart of his lover; as a puisny tilter, that spurs his horse but on one side,

---

statuary (c) chaste — since Diana is goddess of chastity.   **14–15** *of winter's sisterhood* of the coldest order possible [K].   **22** *concave* hollow, insincere.   **23** *covered goblet* A goblet with its ornamental cover on was more "hollow" or "concave" than it would be with the cover off.   **28** *the word of a tapster* There was a general idea that tapsters — waiters who served drinks — were not scrupulous about cheating in the bill rendered [K].   **31** *question* conversation.   **33** *as good* as noble in rank.   **35** *brave* fine.   **37** *traverse* striking the opponent sideways and awkwardly rather than head-on — a term from the sport of tilting.   **38** *puisny* unpractised, unskillful; literally, "younger" (French "puis né," "later born"). It is an older form of "puny" [K].

breaks his staff like a noble goose. But all's brave that
youth mounts and folly guides. Who comes here?   40

Enter Corin.

COR.   Mistress and master, you have oft inquir'd
After the shepherd that complain'd of love,
Who you saw sitting by me on the turf,
Praising the proud disdainful shepherdess
That was his mistress.

CEL.   Well, and what of him?   45

COR.   If you will see a pageant truly play'd
Between the pale complexion of true love
And the red glow of scorn and proud disdain,
Go hence a little, and I shall conduct you,
If you will mark it.

ROS.   O, come, let us remove!   50
The sight of lovers feedeth those in love.
Bring us to this sight, and you shall say
I'll prove a busy actor in their play.   *Exeunt.*

◇◇◇◇◇◇◇◇◇◇◇◇◇◇◇◇◇

SCENE V. [*Another part of the Forest.*]

Enter Silvius *and* Phebe.

SIL.   Sweet Phebe, do not scorn me; do not, Phebe!
Say that you love me not, but say not so
In bitterness. The common executioner,
Whose heart th' accustom'd sight of death makes hard,
Falls not the axe upon the humbled neck   5

---

39 *goose* fool.   41 *Mistress and master* As soon as the conventionally pastoral part
of the drama begins again, the same delicate prettiness of style and metre, already
noted, is resumed [K].   42 *complain'd of* lamented about.   46 *pageant* theatrical
scene.   47 *pale complexion* The lover was pale because each of his sighs, it was
believed, drew a drop of blood from his heart.

  III.v. 5 *Falls not* does not let fall.   6 *begs pardon* It was customary for the
executioner to ask pardon of the condemned man.   7 *dies and lives by bloody*

But first begs pardon. Will you sterner be
Than he that dies and lives by bloody drops?

Enter Rosalind, Celia, *and* Corin, [*be-hind*].

PHE.   I would not be thy executioner.
I fly thee, for I would not injure thee.
Thou tell'st me there is murder in mine eye: 10
'Tis pretty, sure, and very probable
That eyes, that are the frail'st and softest things,
Who shut their coward gates on atomies
Should be call'd tyrants, butchers, murderers!
Now I do frown on thee with all my heart;   15
And if mine eyes can wound, now let them kill thee!
Now counterfeit to swound; why, now fall down;
Or if thou canst not, O, for shame, for shame,
Lie not, to say mine eyes are murderers!
Now show the wound mine eye hath made in thee.   20
Scratch thee but with a pin, and there remains
Some scar of it; lean but upon a rush,
The cicatrice and capable impressure
Thy palm some moment keeps; but now mine eyes,
Which I have darted at thee, hurt thee not,   25
Nor I am sure there is no force in eyes
That can do hurt.

SIL.   O dear Phebe,
If ever (as that ever may be near)
You meet in some fresh cheek the power of fancy,
Then shall you know the wounds invisible   30
That love's keen arrows make.

PHE.   But till that time

---

drops gets his livelihood to the day of his death by shedding blood [K].   9 *for* because.   13 *atomies* motes, specks of dust.   17 *counterfeit to swound* pretend to faint.   19 *to say* by saying. A common loose use of the infinitive [K].   22 *but upon* F²; F¹: "vpon."   23 *cicatrice* literally, "scar"; here merely "mark" [K]. *capable impressure* impression that may be perceived [K].   24 *some moment* for a moment or so.   29 *fresh* the common Elizabethan adjective to describe the bloom of youthful beauty [K]. *fancy* love.

Come not thou near me; and when that time comes,
Afflict me with thy mocks, pity me not,
As till that time I shall not pity thee.

ROS.   And why, I pray you? Who might be your mother,   35
That you insult, exult, and all at once,
Over the wretched? What though you have no beauty —
As, by my faith, I see no more in you
Than without candle may go dark to bed! —
Must you be therefore proud and pitiless?   40
Why, what means this? Why do you look on me?
I see no more in you than in the ordinary
Of Nature's sale-work. 'Od's my little life,
I think she means to tangle my eyes too!
No, faith, proud mistress, hope not after it.   45
'Tis not your inky brows, your black silk hair,
Your bugle eyeballs, nor your cheek of cream
That can entame my spirits to your worship.
You foolish shepherd, wherefore do you follow her,
Like foggy south, puffing with wind and rain?   50
You are a thousand times a properer man
Than she a woman. 'Tis such fools as you
That makes the world full of ill-favour'd children.
'Tis not her glass, but you, that flatters her,
And out of you she sees herself more proper   55
Than any of her lineaments can show her.
But, mistress, know yourself. Down on your knees,
And thank heaven, fasting, for a good man's love;
For I must tell you friendly in your ear,

36 *and all at once* both at the same time.   39 *Than without . . . to bed* I see no
more beauty in you than will force you, unless you have a candle, to go to bed
in the dark, since your beauty is not sufficient to illuminate the night [K].   40
Must you . . . proud grant you are ugly, is that any reason for pride? The taunt
is much more bitter than if Rosalind had granted her "some" beauty [K].   43
Nature's sale-work the ordinary everyday product of Nature's manufacture [K].
'Od's my little life A trivial oath, meaning, literally, "God save my life!" Rosalind
swears in order to maintain her "swashing and martial outside" (I.III.115), but her
oaths are ladylike — "pretty oaths that are not dangerous" (IV.I.163–4) [K].   47
bugle black and beady [K].   *cheek of cream* i.e. of light yellow. Rosalind is con-
temptuously referring to Phebe's brunette complexion [K].   48 *entame . . . worship* subdue my feelings to adoration of you [K].   50 *south* the south wind, which

Sell when you can! you are not for all markets.   60
Cry the man mercy, love him, take his offer.
Foul is most foul, being foul to be a scoffer.
So take her to thee, shepherd. Fare you well.

PHE.   Sweet youth, I pray you chide a year together.
I had rather hear you chide than this man woo.   65

ROS.   [to Phebe] He's fall'n in love with your foulness, [to
Silvius] and she'll fall in love with my anger. If it be so,
as fast as she answers thee with frowning looks, I'll sauce
her with bitter words. — Why look you so upon me?

PHE.   For no ill will I bear you.   70

ROS.   I pray you do not fall in love with me,
For I am falser than vows made in wine.
Besides, I like you not. If you will know my house,
'Tis at the tuft of olives, here hard by. —
Will you go, sister? — Shepherd, ply her hard. —   75
Come, sister. — Shepherdess, look on him better
And be not proud. Though all the world could see,
None could be so abus'd in sight as he. —
Come, to our flock.

                    Exeunt [Rosalind, Celia, *and* Corin].

PHE.   Dead shepherd, now I find thy saw of might,   80
"Who ever lov'd that lov'd not at first sight?"

SIL.   Sweet Phebe —

PHE.   Ha! what say'st thou, Silvius?

---

in Shakespeare's country brings fog and rain [K]. The weeping and sighing of
the lover were conventional.   51 *properer* more handsome.   53 *ill-favour'd* ugly.
54 *glass* mirror.   55 *out of you* as reflected from your opinion of her [K].   *proper*
beautiful.   61 *Cry the man mercy* beg the man's pardon.   62 *Foul . . . a scoffer*
the ugly woman is rendered more ugly when, in spite of her ugliness, she scorns to
love (is a scoffer).   68–9 *sauce her* Sharp sauces to whet the appetite were much
in favour in Shakespeare's time. If the sauce were too sour or too bitter, it
would sting the palate or "set the teeth on edge" [K].   80 *Dead shepherd* Marlowe, the author of the verse quoted, was killed in 1593 [K].   *I find thy saw of
might* I recognize the force of thy saying [K]   81 *Who ever . . . sight* The line
is in HERO AND LEANDER (I.176), published in 1598.

SIL.   Sweet Phebe, pity me.

PHE.   Why, I am sorry for thee, gentle Silvius.

SIL.   Wherever sorrow is, relief would be.   85
        If you do sorrow at my grief in love,
        By giving love your sorrow and my grief
        Were both extermin'd.

PHE.   Thou hast my love. Is not that neighbourly?

SIL.   I would have you.

PHE.   Why, that were covetousness.   90
        Silvius, the time was that I hated thee,
        And yet it is not that I bear thee love;
        But since that thou canst talk of love so well,
        Thy company, which erst was irksome to me,
        I will endure; and I'll employ thee too.   95
        But do not look for further recompense
        Than thine own gladness that thou art employ'd.

SIL.   So holy and so perfect is my love,
        And I in such a poverty of grace,
        That I shall think it a most plenteous crop   100
        To glean the broken ears after the man
        That the main harvest reaps. Loose now and then
        A scatt'red smile, and that I'll live upon.

PHE.   Know'st thou the youth that spoke to me erewhile?

SIL.   Not very well, but I have met him oft,   105
        And he hath bought the cottage and the bounds
        That the old carlot once was master of.

PHE.   Think not I love him, though I ask for him.
        'Tis but a peevish boy; yet he talks well.

---

88 *extermin'd* banished.   89 *neighbourly* as opposed to "conjugal" love. There
may be an allusion to MATTHEW, XIX, 19: "Thou shalt love thy neighbour as thyself."   92 *And yet it is not that* and the time has not yet come when. "Is" bears
the emphasis [K].   94 *erst* formerly.   99 *in such a poverty of grace* in so poverty-
stricken a condition with regard to your favour [K]. The religious imagery is appropriate, for Silvius worships Phebe as a deity.   103 *A scatt'red smile* a stray
smile — let loose, as it were, casually, without any special thought of me. The
figure is from archery [K].   104 *erewhile* a while ago.   107 *carlot* churl, peasant.

But what care I for words? Yet words do well   110
When he that speaks them pleases those that hear.
It is a pretty youth — not very pretty —
But sure he's proud; and yet his pride becomes him.
He'll make a proper man. The best thing in him
Is his complexion; and faster than his tongue   115
Did make offence, his eye did heal it up.
He is not very tall; yet for his years he's tall.
His leg is but so so; and yet 'tis well.
There was a pretty redness in his lip,
A little riper and more lusty red   120
Than that mix'd in his cheek; 'twas just the difference
Betwixt the constant red and mingled damask.
There be some women, Silvius, had they mark'd him
In parcels as I did, would have gone near
To fall in love with him; but, for my part,   125
I love him not nor hate him not; and yet
I have more cause to hate him than to love him;
For what had he to do to chide at me?
He said mine eyes were black and my hair black;
And, now I am rememb'red, scorn'd at me.   130
I marvel why I answer'd not again.
But that's all one: omittance is no quittance.
I'll write to him a very taunting letter,
And thou shalt bear it. Wilt thou, Silvius?

SIL.   Phebe, with all my heart.

PHE.   I'll write it straight;   135
The matter 's in my head and in my heart.
I will be bitter with him and passing short.
Go with me, Silvius.   *Exeunt.*

---

108 *ask for* inquire after.   109 *peevish* childish, silly.   114 *proper* handsome.
122 *constant* uniform, unmixed with other colours.   *mingled damask* blended red
and white — the colour of the damask rose.   124 *In parcels* feature by feature;
literally, piecemeal, in parts [K].   127 *I have* F²: F¹: "Haue."   128 *had he to do*
business had he.   130 *am rememb'red* do remember.   132 *omittance is no quit-*
tance to refrain from asserting one's rights or claims is not to renounce them. A
proverbial bit of legal lore. A "quittance" is a receipt in full of all demands [K].
135 *straight* at once.   137 *passing* surpassingly, extremely.

Act Four

<<<<<<<<<<<<<<<<<<<<<<<<<<<<<<<<<<<<<<<<<<<<<<<<<<<<

SCENE I. [*The Forest. Near the sheepcote.*]

Enter Rosalind *and* Celia *and* Jaques.

JAQ.   I prithee, pretty youth, let me be better acquainted
         with thee.

ROS.   They say you are a melancholy fellow.

JAQ.   I am so. I do love it better than laughing.

ROS.   Those that are in extremity of either are abominable   5
         fellows, and betray themselves to every modern censure
         worse than drunkards.

JAQ.   Why, 'tis good to be sad and say nothing.

ROS.   Why then, 'tis good to be a post.

JAQ.   I have neither the scholar's melancholy, which is emula-   10

IV.I. 5 *are in extremity* go to extremes.   6 *betray themselves . . . modern censure*
make themselves ridiculous, not merely to the wise, but even to persons of ordinary
judgment [K].   *modern* commonplace, ordinary.   8 *sad* serious.   9 *a post* Rosalind
puns on "sad." A post is both sad (i.e. heavy) and dumb [K].   10 *emulation* envy.
Commoner in this sense than in that of "generous rivalry," to which it is now
restricted. Envy has always been regarded as the besetting sin of the learned [K].
11 *is fantastical* is due to an oversensitive fancy or imagination [K].   13 *politic*
The lawyer assumes a melancholy air in order to be regarded as a grave and
profoundly learned counsellor [K].   14 *nice* unduly fastidious. The fine lady is
depressed because the world is too rude for her delicate nerves [K].   16 *simples*
ingredients (which make up a compound). Common as a medical term [K].   *many
objects* many observations that I have made of persons and events [K].   17 *the
sundry contemplation* the contemplation of different particulars, which I have
observed [K].   17–18 *in which . . . sadness* in which my habit of ruminating wraps
me, so that I am in a state of sober thought that is full of humorous (i.e. odd)
fancies, such as do not occur to the thoughtless and inexperienced. The antecedent of "which" is "melancholy" [K].   *my often* F²; F¹: "by often."   27–36 *Good*

76

tion; nor the musician's, which is fantastical; nor the courtier's, which is proud; nor the soldier's, which is ambitious; nor the lawyer's, which is politic; nor the lady's, which is nice; nor the lover's, which is all these: but it is a melancholy of mine own, compounded of 15 many simples, extracted from many objects, and indeed the sundry contemplation of my travels, in which my often rumination wraps me in a most humorous sadness.

ROS.   A traveller! By my faith, you have great reason to be sad. I fear you have sold your own lands to see other 20 men's. Then to have seen much and to have nothing is to have rich eyes and poor hands.

JAQ.   Yes, I have gain'd my experience.

Enter Orlando.

ROS.   And your experience makes you sad. I had rather have a fool to make me merry than experience to make me 25 sad — and to travel for it too!

ORL.   Good day and happiness, dear Rosalind!

JAQ.   Nay then, God buy you, an you talk in blank verse!

ROS.   Farewell, Monsieur Traveller. Look you lisp and wear strange suits, disable all the benefits of your own coun- 30 try, be out of love with your nativity and almost chide

---

day . . . sight more The action has been much discussed but it is plain enough if we remember that exits and entrances were all made through doors at the rear of the stage. When Orlando enters, Jaques and Rosalind are near the front. Jaques begins to retire at line 28, but Rosalind walks with him toward the back of the stage, continuing the conversation in lines 29-33. At line 33 Jaques actually makes his exit. Up to this moment Rosalind has purposely taken no notice of Orlando, who entered, with a greeting "in blank verse," at line 27, and immediately advanced toward the front. Having bidden adieu to Jaques, Rosalind now at the back of the stage, turns round and condescends to address the tardy Orlando, pretending not to have seen him before [K].   28 *God buy you* F¹; K: "God b' wi' you."   29 *Monsieur Traveller* The faults and affectations of Englishmen who had travelled on the Continent were common objects of satire. Rosalind touches on the points usually mentioned [K].   *Look you* see that you.   *lisp* speak with an affected or mincing pronunciation [K].   29-30 *wear strange suits* The fondness of gallants for foreign fashions was often satirized. They were also accused of combining details of the attire of different countries in one tasteless and fantastic costume [K].   *disable* decry, disparage.   31 *nativity* birth and birthplace [K].

God for making you that countenance you are; or I will
scarce think you have swam in a gundello. [*Exit* Jaques.]
Why, how now, Orlando? Where have you been all this
while? You a lover? An you serve me such another trick,   35
never come in my sight more.

ORL.   My fair Rosalind, I come within an hour of my promise.

ROS.   Break an hour's promise in love? He that will divide a
minute into a thousand parts and break but a part of
the thousand part of a minute in the affairs of love, it   40
may be said of him that Cupid hath clapp'd him o' th'
shoulder, but I'll warrant him heart-whole.

ORL.   Pardon me, dear Rosalind.

ROS.   Nay, an you be so tardy, come no more in my sight. I
had as lief be woo'd of a snail.   45

ORL.   Of a snail?

ROS.   Ay, of a snail; for though he comes slowly, he carries his
house on his head — a better jointure, I think, than you
make a woman. Besides, he brings his destiny with him.

ORL.   What's that?   50

ROS.   Why, horns! which such as you are fain to be beholding
to your wives for; but he comes armed in his fortune
and prevents the slander of his wife.

ORL.   Virtue is no horn-maker, and my Rosalind is virtuous.

ROS.   And I am your Rosalind.   55

CEL.   It pleases him to call you so; but he hath a Rosalind of
a better leer than you.

ROS.   Come, woo me, woo me! for now I am in a holiday hu-

---

32 *that countenance you are* with features like those of your own countrymen [K].
33 *gundello* gondola. Venice was, in Shakespeare's time, the gayest and most
fashionable city in Europe [K].   41-2 *clapp'd him o' th' shoulder* given him a
casual greeting. Not "arrested him," which does not fit the context. Love has
touched him, to be sure, but only slightly: his heart has not been affected [K].
48 *jointure* estate settled on a wife for her possession if her husband predeceases
her [K].   51 *beholding* beholden, indebted.   53 *prevents* forestalls; prevents by
anticipating. Since the snail has horns before marriage, no one will be able to
infer from his possessing them that his wife has misconducted herself [K].   57

mour and like enough to consent. What would you say
to me now, an I were your very very Rosalind?   60

ORL.   I would kiss before I spoke.

ROS.   Nay, you were better speak first; and when you were
gravell'd for lack of matter, you might take occasion to
kiss. Very good orators, when they are out, they will spit;
and for lovers, lacking (God warn us!) matter, the clean-   65
liest shift is to kiss.

ORL.   How if the kiss be denied?

ROS.   Then she puts you to entreaty, and there begins new
matter.

ORL.   Who could be out, being before his beloved mistress?   70

ROS.   Marry, that should you, if I were your mistress, or I
should think my honesty ranker than my wit.

ORL.   What, of my suit?

ROS.   Not out of your apparel, and yet out of your suit. Am
not I your Rosalind?   75

ORL.   I take some joy to say you are, because I would be talking of her.

ROS.   Well, in her person, I say I will not have you.

ORL.   Then, in mine own person, I die.

ROS.   No, faith, die by attorney. The poor world is almost six   80
thousand years old, and in all this time there was not
any man died in his own person, videlicet, in a love
cause. Troilus had his brains dash'd out with a Grecian
club; yet he did what he could to die before, and he is

---

leer look, aspect.   63 *gravell'd* disconcerted, stuck (like a ship that has run
aground).   *matter* subject matter.   64 *are out* have had a lapse of memory [K].
65 *warn* warrant, defend.   65-6 *cleanliest shift* most expedient device.   72
honesty chastity.   *ranker* more corrupt, less pure.   80 *by attorney* by proxy.
82 *in his own person* rather than in a story or drama.   83 *Troilus* the ideal of
fidelity in love, as Cressida was a synonym for falseness.   84 *club* Rosalind is
purposely depriving the death of Troilus of all dignity. He was slain by the spear
of Achilles [K].

one of the patterns of love. Leander, he would have liv'd   85
many a fair year though Hero had turn'd nun, if it had
not been for a hot midsummer night; for (good youth)
he went but forth to wash him in the Hellespont, and
being taken with the cramp, was drown'd; and the foolish chroniclers of that age found it was "Hero of Sestos."   90
But these are all lies. Men have died from time to time,
and worms have eaten them, but not for love.

ORL.   I would not have my right Rosalind of this mind, for I
protest her frown might kill me.

ROS.   By this hand, it will not kill a fly! But come, now I will   95
be your Rosalind in a more coming-on disposition; and
ask me what you will, I will grant it.

ORL.   Then love me, Rosalind.

ROS.   Yes, faith, will I, Fridays and Saturdays and all.

ORL.   And wilt thou have me?   100

ROS.   Ay, and twenty such.

ORL.   What sayest thou?

ROS.   Are you not good?

ORL.   I hope so.

ROS.   Why then, can one desire too much of a good thing?   105
Come, sister, you shall be the priest and marry us. Give
me your hand, Orlando. What do you say, sister?

ORL.   Pray thee marry us.

CEL.   I cannot say the words.

ROS.   You must begin, "Will you, Orlando" —   110

CEL.   Go to. Will you, Orlando, have to wife this Rosalind?

85-90 *Leander . . . of Sestos* Leander, another ideal of faithful love, drowned
while swimming the Hellespont from Abydos to Sestos, where his sweetheart
Hero lived. Rosalind mocks him also by implying that he died of a swimmer's
cramp.   117 *commission* authority (for taking her, since there is no one to give
her away).   118 *goes before* runs ahead of.   119-20 *runs before her actions*
moves so fast as to outstrip any regularly settled plan of conduct. Rosalind re-
verses the common saying that women act before they think; but she does not
change its sense thereby [K].   125-6 *Men are April* composed of wind and rain

ORL.   I will.

ROS.   Ay, but when?

ORL.   Why now, as fast as she can marry us.

ROS.   Then you must say, "I take thee, Rosalind, for wife."   115

ORL.   I take thee, Rosalind, for wife.

ROS.   I might ask you for your commission; but I do take thee, Orlando, for my husband. There's a girl goes before the priest, and certainly a woman's thought runs before her actions.   120

ORL.   So do all thoughts; they are wing'd.

ROS.   Now tell me how long you would have her after you have possess'd her.

ORL.   For ever and a day.

ROS.   Say "a day," without the "ever." No, no, Orlando! Men   125 are April when they woo, December when they wed. Maids are May when they are maids, but the sky changes when they are wives. I will be more jealous of thee than a Barbary cock-pigeon over his hen, more clamorous than a parrot against rain, more newfangled than an ape,   130 more giddy in my desires than a monkey. I will weep for nothing, like Diana in the fountain, and I will do that when you are dispos'd to be merry; I will laugh like a hyen, and that when thou art inclin'd to sleep.

ORL.   But will my Rosalind do so?   135

ROS.   By my life, she will do as I do.

ORL.   O, but she is wise!

ROS.   Or else she could not have the wit to do this. The wiser,

---

(sighs and tears). There is probably a suggestion also of youthful ardour, as contrasted with the coldness of December (after marriage).   129 *Barbary cock-pigeon* the kind of pigeon known as the "barb" [K], of oriental origin and supposedly very jealous of its mate.   130 *against rain* before rain; when it is going to rain [K].   *newfangled* fond of novelty.   132 *Diana in the fountain* Fountains made up of weeping Diana (water coming from her eyes and breasts) were quite common.   134 *hyen* hyena, whose bark resembles a laugh.

the waywarder. Make the doors upon a woman's wit, and
it will out at the casement; shut that, and 'twill out at 140
the keyhole; stop that, 'twill fly with the smoke out at
the chimney.

ORL. A man that had a wife with such a wit, he might say,
"Wit, whither wilt?"

ROS. Nay, you might keep that check for it till you met your 145
wife's wit going to your neighbour's bed.

ORL. And what wit could wit have to excuse that?

ROS. Marry, to say she came to seek you there. You shall never
take her without her answer unless you take her without her tongue. O, that woman that cannot make her 150
fault her husband's occasion, let her never nurse her
child herself, for she will breed it like a fool!

ORL. For these two hours, Rosalind, I will leave thee.

ROS. Alas, dear love, I cannot lack thee two hours!

ORL. I must attend the Duke at dinner. By two o'clock I will 155
be with thee again.

ROS. Ay, go your ways, go your ways! I knew what you would
prove. My friends told me as much, and I thought no
less. That flattering tongue of yours won me. 'Tis but
one cast away, and so, come death! Two o'clock is your 160
hour?

ORL. Ay, sweet Rosalind.

ROS. By my troth, and in good earnest, and so God mend me,
and by all pretty oaths that are not dangerous, if you
break one jot of your promise or come one minute be- 165

---

139 *Make* shut.   144 *Wit, whither wilt* A proverbial phrase, here punningly applied by Orlando. It is properly a question addressed to one's own wit (i.e. common sense), and means: "Where are you going, my wits, for you seem to be
leaving me?" It implies, then, that one is talking idly or fantastically [K].   145
check rebuke.   151 *her husband's occasion* an opportunity for finding fault with
her husband — turning the tables on him completely and so putting him in the
wrong [K].   152 *breed it* bring it up.   154 *lack thee* bear to be apart from
thee.   160 *one cast away* one person abandoned.   163 *mend me* amend me; mend
my fortunes.   166 *pathetical* piteous, distressing [K].   167 *hollow* insincere.

hind your hour, I will think you the most pathetical break-promise, and the most hollow lover, and the most unworthy of her you call Rosalind, that may be chosen out of the gross band of the unfaithful. Therefore beware my censure and keep your promise.   170

ORL. With no less religion than if thou wert indeed my Rosalind. So adieu.

ROS. Well, Time is the old justice that examines all such offenders, and let Time try. Adieu.   *Exit* [Orlando].

CEL. You have simply misus'd our sex in your love-prate. We   175
must have your doublet and hose pluck'd over your head, and show the world what the bird hath done to her own nest.

ROS. O coz, coz, coz, my pretty little coz, that thou didst know how many fathom deep I am in love! But it can-   180
not be sounded. My affection hath an unknown bottom, like the Bay of Portugal.

CEL. Or rather, bottomless, that as fast as you pour affection in, it runs out.

ROS. No, that same wicked bastard of Venus that was begot   185
of thought, conceiv'd of spleen, and born of madness, that blind rascally boy that abuses every one's eyes because his own are out — let him be judge how deep I am in love. I'll tell thee, Aliena, I cannot be out of the sight of Orlando. I'll go find a shadow, and sigh till he   190
come.

CEL. And I'll sleep.   *Exeunt.*

---

169 *gross band* whole huge company.   170 *censure* condemnation.   171 *With no less religion* no less religiously, scrupulously.   173 *Time . . . justice* The adage is "Time tries (i.e. tests) all things" [K].   175 *misus'd* abused, slandered. 177–8 *bird . . . nest* A reference to another old proverb: "A foul bird defiles its own nest." There is a play on "bird's nest" as common slang for "pudendum." 182 *Bay of Portugal* known proverbially for the extreme depth of its water.   184 *in, it* F²; F¹: "in, in."   185 *bastard of Venus* Cupid, the son of Venus and Mars. 186 *thought* melancholy. *spleen* mere impulse [K].   187 *abuses* deceives.   190 *shadow* shady spot.

◇◇◇◇◇◇◇◇◇◇◇◇◇◇◇

SCENE II.
[*The Forest. Before* Duke Senior's *cave.*]

Enter Jaques, *and* Lords ([*like*] Foresters) [*with a dead deer*].

JAQ.   Which is he that killed the deer?

LORD.   Sir, it was I.

JAQ.   Let's present him to the Duke like a Roman conqueror;
         and it would do well to set the deer's horns upon his
         head for a branch of victory. Have you no song, forester,   5
         for this purpose?

LORD.   Yes, sir.

JAQ.   Sing it. 'Tis no matter how it be in tune, so it make
         noise enough.   *Music.*

                         Song.

              What shall he have that kill'd the deer?   10
              His leather skin and horns to wear.
                   Then sing him home.

                   (*The rest shall bear this burden.*)

              Take thou no scorn to wear the horn;
              It was a crest ere thou wast born:
                   Thy father's father wore it,   15
                   And thy father bore it.
              The horn, the horn, the lusty horn,
              Is not a thing to laugh to scorn.   *Exeunt.*

IV.II. 3 *like a Roman conqueror* in a triumphal procession [K].   5 *branch of
victory* triumphal garland.   12 s.d. *The rest . . . burden* i.e. sing this refrain or
chorus (THEOBALD; F¹ includes this line as part of the song rather than as a stage
direction, and this may well be correct. "Burden" may refer to "the horns" as well as
to "the chorus").   13 *Take thou no scorn* do not consider it a disgrace. Elizabethans
never tired of jokes about the horns of the cuckold.   14 *crest* (a) head-gear (b)

❖❖❖❖❖❖❖❖❖❖❖❖❖❖

SCENE III. [*The Forest. Near the sheepcote.*]

Enter Rosalind *and* Celia.

ROS. How say you now? Is it not past two o'clock? and here
        much Orlando!

CEL. I warrant you, with pure love and troubled brain, he
        hath ta'en his bow and arrows, and is gone forth to sleep.

Enter Silvius.

        Look who comes here.   5

SIL. My errand is to you, fair youth.
        My gentle Phebe bid me give you this.   [*Gives a letter.*]
        I know not the contents; but, as I guess
        By the stern brow and waspish action
        Which she did use as she was writing of it,   10
        It bears an angry tenure. Pardon me;
        I am but as a guiltless messenger.

ROS. Patience herself would startle at this letter
        And play the swaggerer. Bear this, bear all!
        She says I am not fair, that I lack manners;   15
        She calls me proud, and that she could not love me,
        Were man as rare as phœnix. 'Od's my will!
        Her love is not the hare that I do hunt.
        Why writes she so to me? Well, shepherd, well,
        This is a letter of your own device.   20

SIL. No, I protest, I know not the contents.
        Phebe did write it.

ROS.   Come, come, you are a fool,

---

heraldic sign upon a coat of arms.   17 *lusty* (a) vigorous, flourishing [K] (b)
lustful.

     IV.III. 2 *much Orlando* not much of Orlando! A common ironical use of
"much" [K].   7 *bid* F²; F¹: "did bid."   11 *tenure* tenour, purport.   17 *phœnix*
There was believed to be but one phœnix in the world at a time [K].

And turn'd into the extremity of love.
I saw her hand. She has a leathern hand,
A freestone-coloured hand. I verily did think   25
That her old gloves were on, but 'twas her hands.
She has a housewife's hand; but that's no matter.
I say she never did invent this letter;
This is a man's invention and his hand.

SIL.   Sure it is hers.   30

ROS.   Why, 'tis a boisterous and a cruel style,
A style for challengers. Why, she defies me
Like Turk to Christian! Women's gentle brain
Could not drop forth such giant-rude invention,
Such Ethiop words, blacker in their effect   35
Than in their countenance. Will you hear the letter?

SIL.   So please you, for I never heard it yet —
Yet heard too much of Phebe's cruelty.

ROS.   She Phebes me. Mark how the tyrant writes.   *Read.*

       "Art thou god to shepherd turn'd,   40
         That a maiden's heart hath burn'd?"

Can a woman rail thus?

SIL.   Call you this railing?

ROS.

       "Why, thy godhead laid apart,   *Read.*
         Warr'st thou with a woman's heart?"   45

Did you ever hear such railing?
       "Whiles the eye of man did woo me,
         That could do no vengeance to me."

---

23 *turn'd . . . love* become, as it were, the personification of one who loves beyond all reasonable bounds [K].   25 *freestone-coloured* yellowish brown (like soft sandstone).   29 *hand* handwriting.   33 *Like Turk* because of the savage language she uses [K].   34 *giant-rude* monstrously uncivil.   35 *Ethiop* black. *their effect* what they signify.   36 *countenance* actual appearance.   39 *Phebes me* addresses me in the characteristic Phebe style, as described by you [K].   44 *thy godhead laid apart* having laid thy divinity aside, i.e. assumed human form.   48 *vengeance* harm.   49 *Meaning me a beast* implying that I am inhuman — not a man but a brute [K].   50 *eyne* eyes. Old plural, archaic even in Shakespeare's time [K].   53 *in mild aspect* if they looked upon me gently. "Aspect" is an

Meaning me a beast.

> "If the scorn of your bright eyne   50
> Have power to raise such love in mine,
> Alack, in me what strange effect
> Would they work in mild aspect!
> Whiles you chid me, I did love;
> How then might your prayers move!   55
> He that brings this love to thee
> Little knows this love in me;
> And by him seal up thy mind,
> Whether that thy youth and kind
> Will the faithful offer take   60
> Of me and all that I can make,
> Or else by him my love deny,
> And then I'll study how to die."

SIL.   Call you this chiding?

CEL.   Alas, poor shepherd!   65

ROS.   Do you pity him? No, he deserves no pity. Wilt thou
love such a woman? What, to make thee an instrument,
and play false strains upon thee? Not to be endur'd!
Well, go your way to her (for I see love hath made thee
a tame snake) and say this to her: that if she love me,   70
I charge her to love thee; if she will not, I will never
have her unless thou entreat for her. If you be a true
lover, hence, and not a word; for here comes more company.   *Exit* Silvius.

Enter Oliver.

astrological term denoting the way in which a planet looks upon a man (i.e. with
good or bad effect); hence it is practically synonymous with the "influence" of
the planets. The accent was regularly on the second syllable [K].   58 *by him
seal up thy mind* send by him, in a sealed letter, thy feelings and intentions [K].
59 *kind* nature. Since he is young, his nature, she thinks, may be prone to love
[K].   61 *me and . . . make* myself and all that I can amount to — all that I
have and am [K].   67 *instrument* (a) agent, tool (b) musical instrument.   70
snake Often used, especially in the phrase "poor snake," to express pity or contempt [K].   71 *charge* command.

OLI.   Good morrow, fair ones. Pray you, if you know,   75
        Where in the purlieus of this forest stands
        A sheepcote, fenc'd about with olive trees?

CEL.   West of this place, down in the neighbour bottom.
        The rank of osiers by the murmuring stream
        Left on your right hand brings you to the place.   80
        But at this hour the house doth keep itself;
        There's none within.

OLI.   If that an eye may profit by a tongue,
        Then should I know you by description —
        Such garments and such years: "The boy is fair,   85
        Of female favour, and bestows himself
        Like a ripe sister; the woman low,
        And browner than her brother." Are not you
        The owner of the house I did inquire for?

CEL.   It is no boast, being ask'd, to say we are.   90

OLI.   Orlando doth commend him to you both,
        And to that youth he calls his Rosalind
        He sends this bloody napkin. Are you he?

ROS.   I am. What must we understand by this?

OLI.   Some of my shame, if you will know of me   95
        What man I am, and how, and why, and where
        This handkercher was stain'd.

CEL.   I pray you tell it.

OLI.   When last the young Orlando parted from you,
        He left a promise to return again
        Within an hour; and pacing through the forest,   100
        Chewing the food of sweet and bitter fancy,

---

76 *in the purlieus* within the borders.   78 *neighbour bottom* nearby dale.   79
rank of osiers row of willows.   81 *keep itself* take care of itself — is empty.
83 *profit* learn.   86 *favour* features.   86–7 *bestows himself . . . sister* behaves
like a grown-up elder sister rather than like a brother [K]. Some editors read
"forester" for "sister," a plausible emendation.   88 *browner* darker in complexion.   91 *doth commend him* sends his greetings.   93 *napkin* handkerchief.
97 *handkercher* A proper form in Shakespeare's time [K].   100 *Within an hour*
It was really two hours (see IV.i.154), and so HANMER would read. Probably this

Lo, what befell! He threw his eye aside,
And mark what object did present itself.
Under an old oak, whose boughs were moss'd with age
And high top bald with dry antiquity,   105
A wretched ragged man, o'ergrown with hair,
Lay sleeping on his back. About his neck
A green and gilded snake had wreath'd itself,
Who with her head, nimble in threats, approach'd
The opening of his mouth; but suddenly,   110
Seeing Orlando, it unlink'd itself
And with indented glides did slip away
Into a bush, under which bush's shade
A lioness, with udders all drawn dry,
Lay couching, head on ground, with catlike watch   115
When that the sleeping man should stir; for 'tis
The royal disposition of that beast
To prey on nothing that doth seem as dead.
This seen, Orlando did approach the man
And found it was his brother, his elder brother.   120

CEL.   O, I have heard him speak of that same brother,
And he did render him the most unnatural
That liv'd amongst men.

OLI.   And well he might so do,
For well I know he was unnatural.

ROS.   But, to Orlando! Did he leave him there,   125
Food to the suck'd and hungry lioness?

OLI.   Twice did he turn his back and purpos'd so;
But kindness, nobler ever than revenge,
And nature, stronger than his just occasion,
Made him give battle to the lioness,   130

---

is merely a slip of Shakespeare's pen or memory [K].   101 *fancy* imagination,
probably, rather than "love" [K].   104 *an old oak* F¹; POPE, K: "an oak."   108
snake The lion is in Lodge's novel, but the snake is Shakespeare's contribution
[K].   112 *indented* sinuous, winding.   114 *with udders . . . dry* therefore savage
with hunger.   115 *couching* crouched.   122 *render him* describe him as.   128
kindness instinctive affection [K].   129 *just occasion* good opportunity (for revenge against his brother).

	Who quickly fell before him; in which hurtling	
	From miserable slumber I awak'd.	
CEL.	Are you his brother?	
ROS.	Was it you he rescu'd?	
CEL.	Was't you that did so oft contrive to kill him?	
OLI.	'Twas I. But 'tis not I! I do not shame	135

OLI. 'Twas I. But 'tis not I! I do not shame   135
To tell you what I was, since my conversion
So sweetly tastes, being the thing I am.

ROS. But, for the bloody napkin?

OLI.   By-and-by.
When from the first to last, betwixt us two,
Tears our recountments had most kindly bath'd,   140
As how I came into that desert place —
In brief, he led me to the gentle Duke,
Who gave me fresh array and entertainment,
Committing me unto my brother's love,
Who led me instantly unto his cave,   145
There stripp'd himself, and here upon his arm
The lioness had torn some flesh away,
Which all this while had bled; and now he fainted,
And cried, in fainting, upon Rosalind.
Brief, I recover'd him, bound up his wound;   150
And after some small space, being strong at heart,
He sent me hither, stranger as I am,
To tell this story, that you might excuse
His broken promise, and to give this napkin,
Dy'd in his blood, unto the shepherd youth   155
That he in sport doth call his Rosalind.

                            [Rosalind *swoons*.]

---

131 *hurtling* tumult. 134 *contrive* plot. 136 *my conversion* The conversion is equally sudden in Lodge's novel, in which Saladyne fails to recognize his brother and makes a full confession of his sins to his unknown rescuer. Then Orlando reveals his identity. Such sudden conversions are the regular thing in old plays [K]. They are conventional in romance, and particularly in pastoral romance, with its theme of the power of nature to transform evil. 138 *for* what about. *By-and-by* immediately. 140 *our recountments* our stories told to one another [K]. 141 *As* as, for example — referring back to "recountments." How Oliver "came into that desert place" is the only incident in the recountments that is not already familiar to Rosalind and Celia [K]. 143 *array and entertainment* clothes and food. 150 *recover'd him* brought him back to consciousness

CEL.	Why, how now, Ganymede? sweet Ganymede!
OLI.	Many will swoon when they do look on blood.
CEL.	There is more in it. Cousin Ganymede!
OLI.	Look, he recovers. 160
ROS.	I would I were at home.
CEL.	We'll lead you thither. I pray you, will you take him by the arm?
OLI.	Be of good cheer, youth. You a man? You lack a man's heart.
ROS.	I do so, I confess it. Ah, sirrah, a body would think this 165 was well counterfeited! I pray you tell your brother how well I counterfeited. Heigh-ho!
OLI.	This was not counterfeit. There is too great testimony in your complexion that it was a passion of earnest.
ROS.	Counterfeit, I assure you. 170
OLI.	Well then, take a good heart and counterfeit to be a man.
ROS.	So I do; but, i' faith, I should have been a woman by right.
CEL.	Come, you look paler and paler. Pray you draw home- 175 wards. Good sir, go with us.
OLI.	That will I; for I must bear answer back How you excuse my brother, Rosalind.
ROS.	I shall devise something. But I pray you commend my counterfeiting to him. Will you go? *Exeunt.* 180

[K]. 151 *being strong at heart* when his vital powers had rallied well [K]. 155 *his blood* F²; F¹: "this blood." 159 *Cousin* Though Celia remembers to call Rosalind by her assumed name (Ganymede) here and in line 157, yet, in her distress at Rosalind's swoon, she forgets herself so far as to call her "cousin" instead of "brother." Though "cousin" was used for almost any relative, yet it was not common between brothers and sisters. Johnson's punctuation — "cousin — Ganymed!" is not improbable [K]. 164 *lack* (a) do not have (b) need, desire to have. 169 *a passion of earnest* a genuine swoon. "Passion" is used for any kind of paroxysm, mental or physical [K]. 179–80 *commend my counterfeiting to him* tell him how well I pretended (to faint).

Act Five

◇◇

SCENE I. [*The Forest. Near the sheepcote.*]

Enter [Touchstone the] Clown *and* Audrey.

TOUCH. We shall find a time, Audrey. Patience, gentle Audrey.

AUD. Faith, the priest was good enough, for all the old gentleman's saying.

TOUCH. A most wicked Sir Oliver, Audrey, a most vile Martext! But, Audrey, there is a youth here in the forest lays 5 claim to you.

AUD. Ay, I know who 'tis. He hath no interest in me in the world. Here comes the man you mean.

Enter William.

TOUCH. It is meat and drink to me to see a clown. By my troth, we that have good wits have much to answer for. We 10 shall be flouting; we cannot hold.

WILL. Good ev'n, Audrey.

AUD. God ye good ev'n, William.

WILL. And good ev'n to you, sir.

TOUCH. Good ev'n, gentle friend. Cover thy head, cover thy 15 head. Nay, prithee be cover'd. How old are you, friend?

WILL. Five-and-twenty, sir.

TOUCH. A ripe age. Is thy name William?

V.I. 2–3 *the old gentleman's* A suggestion of Jaques's age, but "old" may signify no more than "elderly" [K].   9 *clown* rustic, yokel.   10–11 *We shall be flouting*

WILL.   William, sir.

TOUCH.   A fair name. Wast born i' th' forest here?   20

WILL.   Ay, sir, I thank God.

TOUCH.   "Thank God." A good answer. Art rich?

WILL.   Faith, sir, so so.

TOUCH.   "So so" is good, very good, very excellent good; and yet
it is not, it is but so so. Art thou wise?   25

WILL.   Ay, sir, I have a pretty wit.

TOUCH.   Why, thou say'st well. I do now remember a saying,
"The fool doth think he is wise, but the wise man knows
himself to be a fool." The heathen philosopher, when
he had a desire to eat a grape, would open his lips when   30
he put it into his mouth, meaning thereby that grapes
were made to eat and lips to open. You do love this
maid?

WILL.   I do, sir.

TOUCH.   Give me your hand. Art thou learned?   35

WILL.   No, sir.

TOUCH.   Then learn this of me: to have is to have; for it is a
figure in rhetoric that drink, being pour'd out of a cup
into a glass, by filling the one doth empty the other; for
all your writers do consent that *ipse* is he. Now, you are   40
not *ipse,* for I am he.

WILL.   Which he, sir?

TOUCH.   He, sir, that must marry this woman. Therefore, you
clown, abandon (which is in the vulgar, leave) the society (which in the boorish is, company) of this female   45
(which in the common is, woman); which together is,
abandon the society of this female, or, clown, thou per-
ishest; or, to thy better understanding, diest; or, to wit,

we are sure to make fun of people [ĸ].   11 *hold* hold back, restrain ourselves.
13 *God ye good ev'n* God give you good evening.   40 *ipse.* Latin for "he himself."

I kill thee, make thee away, translate thy life into death, thy liberty into bondage. I will deal in poison with 50 thee, or in bastinado, or in steel. I will bandy with thee in faction; I will o'errun thee with policy; I will kill thee a hundred and fifty ways. Therefore tremble and depart.

AUD.   Do, good William.   55

WILL.   God rest you merry, sir.   *Exit.*

                    Enter Corin.

COR.   Our master and mistress seeks you. Come away, away!

TOUCH. Trip, Audrey! trip, Audrey! I attend, I attend.

                                            Exeunt.

◆◆◆◆◆◆◆◆◆◆◆◆◆◆◆◆

SCENE II. [*The Forest. Near the sheepcote.*]

Enter Orlando *and* Oliver.

ORL.   Is't possible that on so little acquaintance you should like her? that but seeing, you should love her? and loving, woo? and wooing, she should grant? And will you persever to enjoy her?

OLI.   Neither call the giddiness of it in question, the poverty 5 of her, the small acquaintance, my sudden wooing, nor her sudden consenting; but say with me, I love Aliena;

---

49 *translate* transform.   51 *bastinado* beating with sticks.   51-2 *bandy with thee in faction* engage in party strife with thee. "To bandy" is literally to knock to and fro, like a tennis ball. "Faction" was constantly used for "political party," without the modern implication of disorder or sedition [K].   52 *o'errun thee with policy* outstrip (overcome) thee by means of statecraft. "Policy" is used in the dignified sense and carries out the threat made in the preceding sentence [K]. 56 *rest you merry* keep you in good spirits. A common form of greeting or farewell. William has no perception that Touchstone is "making merry" with him. The threats are serious to him in proportion to their unintelligibility [K].   57 *seeks* A singular verb with two closely associated subjects is very common [K].

 V.II. 5 *giddiness* the dizzy rapidity of the whole affair [K].   11 *estate* settle.

say with her that she loves me; consent with both that
we may enjoy each other. It shall be to your good; for
my father's house, and all the revenue that was old Sir   10
Rowland's, will I estate upon you, and here live and die
a shepherd.

Enter Rosalind.

ORL.   You have my consent. Let your wedding be to-morrow.
Thither will I invite the Duke and all's contented followers. Go you and prepare Aliena; for look you, here   15
comes my Rosalind.

ROS.   God save you, brother.

OLI.   And you, fair sister.   [*Exit.*]

ROS.   O my dear Orlando, how it grieves me to see thee wear
thy heart in a scarf!   20

ORL.   It is my arm.

ROS.   I thought thy heart had been wounded with the claws
of a lion.

ORL.   Wounded it is, but with the eyes of a lady.

ROS.   Did your brother tell you how I counterfeited to sound   25
when he show'd me your handkercher?

ORL.   Ay, and greater wonders than that.

ROS.   O, I know where you are! Nay, 'tis true. There was
never anything so sudden but the fight of two rams and
Cæsar's thrasonical brag of "I came, saw, and overcame."   30
For your brother and my sister no sooner met but they

---

14 *all's* all his. *contented* The contentment which the Duke and his followers
find in their forest life is, as it were, the atmosphere of the whole play (cf. II.1.1–
17). Possibly Orlando makes a mental reservation as to Jaques, the malcontent [K].
18 *sister* Since Rosalind, supposed to be a boy acting the part of Orlando's be-
trothed, calls Oliver "brother," he calls her "sister." We are not to suppose that
he suspects that she is a girl or that Celia has betrayed her cousin's secret [K].
20 *heart in a scarf* Since he has worn his heart on his sleeve and since his arm
is now wounded, she says that his heart is in a surgical dressing (scarf).   25 *sound*
swoon.   28 *where you are* what you mean.   30 *thrasonical* vainglorious, like
the braggart soldier Thraso in Terence's comedy, EUNUCHUS [K].   *overcame* F²; F¹:
"ouercome."

look'd; no sooner look'd but they lov'd; no sooner lov'd
but they sigh'd; no sooner sigh'd but they ask'd one another the reason; no sooner knew the reason but they
sought the remedy: and in these degrees have they made 35
a pair of stairs to marriage, which they will climb incontinent, or else be incontinent before marriage. They
are in the very wrath of love, and they will together.
Clubs cannot part them.

ORL.   They shall be married to-morrow, and I will bid the 40
Duke to the nuptial. But, O, how bitter a thing it is to
look into happiness through another man's eyes! By so
much the more shall I to-morrow be at the height of
heart-heaviness, by how much I shall think my brother
happy in having what he wishes for. 45

ROS.   Why then, to-morrow I cannot serve your turn for
Rosalind?

ORL.   I can live no longer by thinking.

ROS.   I will weary you then no longer with idle talking. Know
of me then (for now I speak to some purpose) that I 50
know you are a gentleman of good conceit. I speak not
this that you should bear a good opinion of my knowledge, insomuch I say I know you are; neither do I
labour for a greater esteem than may in some little
measure draw a belief from you, to do yourself good, 55
and not to grace me. Believe then, if you please, that
I can do strange things. I have, since I was three year
old, convers'd with a magician, most profound in his
art and yet not damnable. If you do love Rosalind so

---

35 *degrees* An obvious pun on the literal meaning of "degree": "step" [K].   36–7
incontinent immediately.   37 *be incontinent* be unchaste.   38 *wrath* passion.
39 *Clubs* These were the regular weapons of London journeymen and apprentices.
The cry "Clubs!" was their watchword, whether in raising a riot or in rallying
to keep the peace [K].   48 *by thinking* merely by imagining (happiness), rather
than actually experiencing it.   51 *conceit* power of conception, intelligence.   52
that so that.   53 *insomuch I say* inasmuch as I say.   56 *grace me* get credit for
myself.   58 *convers'd* associated.   59 *not damnable* Rosalind means that he
practised only such magic as depended on an acquaintance with occult laws of
nature, and that the spirits he invoked were those of the elements — not evil
demons. Such was Prospero's magic in THE TEMPEST [K].   60 *gesture cries it out*

near the heart as your gesture cries it out, when your   60
brother marries Aliena shall you marry her. I know into
what straits of fortune she is driven; and it is not impossible to me, if it appear not inconvenient to you, to
set her before your eyes to-morrow human as she is, and
without any danger.   65

ORL.   Speak'st thou in sober meanings?

ROS.   By my life, I do! which I tender dearly, though I say I
am a magician. Therefore put you in your best array,
bid your friends; for if you will be married to-morrow,
you shall; and to Rosalind, if you will.   70

Enter Silvius *and* Phebe.

Look, here comes a lover of mine and a lover of hers.

PHE.   Youth, you have done me much ungentleness
To show the letter that I writ to you.

ROS.   I care not if I have. It is my study
To seem despiteful and ungentle to you.   75
You are there followed by a faithful shepherd.
Look upon him, love him; he worships you.

PHE.   Good shepherd, tell this youth what 'tis to love.

SIL.   It is to be all made of sighs and tears;
And so am I for Phebe.   80

PHE.   And I for Ganymede.

ORL.   And I for Rosalind.

ROS.   And I for no woman.

---

bearing proclaims.   63 *inconvenient* improper (as being the result of magic arts).
To practise any kind of magic exposed one to suspicion of dealing with evil
spirits [K].   65 *danger* Black magic (the "damnable" kind) was thought to be
very dangerous to the practiser and the spectator. The spirits that were raised
might escape from the magician's control and do mischief [K].   67 *tender dearly*
value highly. Since the practice of magic was punishable by death, Rosalind
may be hinting that she is not really a magician.   67-8 *though I say I am a
magician* though I seem to risk it by confessing that I practise magic [K].   72 *ungentleness* ungentlemanly conduct, discourtesy. Rosalind turns the world, however, so that her "ungentle" (line 75) means "unkind" [K].

SIL.	It is to be all made of faith and service;
	And so am I for Phebe.	85
PHE.	And I for Ganymede.
ORL.	And I for Rosalind.
ROS.	And I for no woman.
SIL.	It is to be all made of fantasy,
	All made of passion, and all made of wishes,	90
	All adoration, duty, and observance,
	All humbleness, all patience, and impatience,
	All purity, all trial, all observance;
	And so am I for Phebe.
PHE.	And so am I for Ganymede.	95
ORL.	And so am I for Rosalind.
ROS.	And so am I for no woman.
PHE.	[*to* Rosalind] If this be so, why blame you me to love you?
SIL.	[*to* Phebe] If this be so, why blame you me to love you?	100
ORL.	If this be so, why blame you me to love you?
ROS.	Who do you speak to, "Why blame you me to love you?"
ORL.	To her that is not here, nor doth not hear.
ROS.	Pray you, no more of this; 'tis like the howling of Irish wolves against the moon. [*To* Silvius] I will help you if	105
	I can. — [*To* Phebe] I would love you if I could. — To-
	morrow meet me all together. — [*To* Phebe] I will marry
	you if ever I marry woman, and I'll be married to-
	morrow. — [*To* Orlando] I will satisfy you if ever I satis-
	fied man, and you shall be married to-morrow. — [*To*	110
	Silvius] I will content you if what pleases you contents

89 *fantasy* fancy (not "love" in this instance).   91 *observance* devotion.   93 *all trial* capable of any test of love.   *observance* F¹; MALONE, K: "obedience." The emendation has been widely accepted on the supposition that the F¹ compositor inadvertently repeated "observance" from line 91; but "obedience" is a singularly weak word here, and there is no real justification for departure from the F¹ text. 98-9 *to love you* for loving you.   104-5 *Irish wolves* The wolf was not extinct in Ireland until long after Shakespeare wrote [K]. There is thus little reason to

you, and you shall be married to-morrow. — [*To* Or-
lando] As you love Rosalind, meet. — [*To* Silvius] As
you love Phebe, meet. — And as I love no woman, I'll
meet. So fare you well. I have left you commands. 115

SIL. I'll not fail if I live.

PHE. Nor I.

ORL. Nor I. *Exeunt.*

◇◇◇◇◇◇◇◇◇◇◇◇◇◇◇◇

S C E N E I I I . [*The Forest. Near the sheepcote.*]

Enter [Touchstone the] Clown *and* Audrey.

TOUCH. To-morrow is the joyful day, Audrey; to-morrow will we
be married.

AUD. I do desire it with all my heart; and I hope it is no
dishonest desire to desire to be a woman of the world.
Here comes two of the banish'd Duke's pages. 5

Enter two Pages.

1. PAGE. Well met, honest gentleman.

TOUCH. By my troth, well met. Come, sit, sit, and a song!

2. PAGE. We are for you. Sit i' th' middle.

1. PAGE. Shall we clap into't roundly, without hawking or spit-
ting or saying we are hoarse, which are the only pro- 10
logues to a bad voice?

2. PAGE. I' faith, i 'faith! and both in a tune, like two gypsies on
a horse.

suppose this a reference to the Irish rebellion of 1598, as has been suggested, the
"wolves" being the rebels, and the "moon" being the virgin queen, Elizabeth.
V.III. 4 *dishonest* dishonourable, immodest. Not quite so strong as "unchaste"
[K]. *woman of the world* married woman. To "go to the world" was a common
idiom for to "get married" [K]. 8 *for you* prepared to serve you. 9 *clap into't
roundly* dash into it vigorously — without ceremony or delay [K]. 12 *in a tune*
in the same tune. 13 *a horse* the same horse.

Song.

It was a lover and his lass —
   With a hey, and a ho, and a hey nonino —   15
That o'er the green cornfield did pass
   In springtime, the only pretty ring-time,
When birds do sing, hey ding a ding, ding.
Sweet lovers love the spring.

Between the acres of the rye —   20
   With a hey, and a ho, and a hey nonino —
These pretty country folks would lie
   In springtime, &c.

This carol they began that hour —
   With a hey, and a ho, and a hey nonino —   25
How that a life was but a flower
   In springtime, &c.

And therefore take the present time —
   With a hey, and a ho, and a hey nonino —
For love is crowned with the prime   30
   In springtime, &c.

TOUCH. Truly, young gentlemen, though there was no great
matter in the ditty, yet the note was very untuneable.

1. PAGE. You are deceiv'd, sir. We kept time, we lost not our
time.   35

TOUCH. By my troth, yes! I count it but time lost to hear such
a foolish song. Good buy you, and God mend your
voices! Come, Audrey.   *Exeunt.*

---

14 *It was a lover and his lass* The song, with music, is given by Thomas Morley
in THE FIRST BOOKE OF AYRES, 1600 (ed. Fellowes, pp. 26–8). The order of stanzas
in the text follows Morley. In F¹ the fourth stanza comes second [K]. 17 *spring-time* MORLEY; F¹: "the spring time." *ring-time* time for wedding rings (MORLEY;
F¹: "rang time"). 20 *Between the acres* on the balks or strips of unploughed turf
that divide the several acre-lots of the ryefield [K]. 22 *folks* F¹: MORLEY: "fooles."
28 *And therefore . . . time* F¹; MORLEY: "Then prettie louers take the time."

◇◇◇◇◇◇◇◇◇◇◇◇◇◇◇◇

SCENE IV. [*The Forest. Near the sheepcote.*]

Enter Duke Senior, Amiens, Jaques, Orlando, Oliver,
Celia.

DUKE S. Dost thou believe, Orlando, that the boy
Can do all this that he hath promised?

ORL. I sometimes do believe, and sometimes do not,
As those that fear they hope, and know they fear.

Enter Rosalind, Silvius, *and* Phebe.

ROS. Patience once more, whiles our compact is urg'd.   5
You say, if I bring in your Rosalind,
You will bestow her on Orlando here?

DUKE S. That would I, had I kingdoms to give with her.

ROS. And you say you will have her when I bring her?

ORL. That would I, were I of all kingdoms king.   10

ROS. You say you'll marry me, if I be willing?

PHE. That will I, should I die the hour after.

ROS. But if you do refuse to marry me,
You'll give yourself to this most faithful shepherd?

PHE. So is the bargain.   15

ROS. You say that you'll have Phebe, if she will?

SIL. Though to have her and death were both one thing.

ROS. I have promis'd to make all this matter even.

---

take seize for enjoyment [K].   30 *the prime* the spring.   33 *ditty* words of the
song. *note . . . untuneable* the tune was untuneful, discordant.   37 *God buy* F¹;
K: "God b' wi'."

V.IV. 4 *fear they hope* feel fear at the very thought of hoping, so much that
they dread the bitterness of disappointment [K].   5 *compact is urg'd* agreement
is rehearsed.   18 *make all this matter even* remove all the difficulties or ob-
structions that beset it [K].

Keep you your word, O Duke, to give your daughter;
You yours, Orlando, to receive his daughter;   20
Keep your word, Phebe, that you'll marry me,
Or else, refusing me, to wed this shepherd;
Keep your word, Silvius, that you'll marry her
If she refuse me; and from hence I go,
To make these doubts all even.   25

Exeunt Rosalind *and* Celia.

DUKE S.   I do remember in this shepherd boy
           Some lively touches of my daughter's favour.

ORL.   My lord, the first time that I ever saw him
           Methought he was a brother to your daughter.
           But, my good lord, this boy is forest-born,   30
           And hath been tutor'd in the rudiments
           Of many desperate studies by his uncle,
           Whom he reports to be a great magician,
           Obscured in the circle of this forest.

Enter [Touchstone the] Clown *and*
Audrey.

JAQ.   There is, sure, another flood toward, and these couples 35
           are coming to the ark. Here comes a pair of very strange
           beasts, which in all tongues are call'd fools.

TOUCH.   Salutation and greeting to you all!

JAQ.   Good my lord, bid him welcome. This is the motley-

21 *Keep your* POPE; F¹: "Keep you your."   25 *doubts all even* questionable matters clear and plain.   27 *lively touches* lifelike traits. *favour* features.   32
desperate perilous — as the practice of any kind of magic was thought to be [K].
34 *Obscured* hidden, living in retirement. *circle of this forest* There may be
an allusion to the magic circle used in conjuring. While within the circle the
magician was safe from devils. Here the entire forest is conceived of as the
circle in which the magician safely practises his art.   35 *toward* coming on.
38 *Salutation and greeting* From his superb entry to his sententious "Much virtue
in If" (which has become a proverb) Touchstone is unapproachable in this scene.
He is among courtiers and noblemen, and he utters the most "admirable fooling"
that the greatest of dramatists could devise [K].   42 *put me to my purgation* call
upon me to clear myself (of the suspicion of lying); put me to the test [K].   43
trod a measure danced.   44 *politic* crafty.   45 *undone* ruined financially.   46
like to have fought came near to fighting.   47 *ta'en up* settled without a duel.

minded gentleman that I have so often met in the 40
forest. He hath been a courtier, he swears.

TOUCH. If any man doubt that, let him put me to my purgation.
I have trod a measure; I have flatt'red a lady; I have
been politic with my friend, smooth with mine enemy;
I have undone three tailors; I have had four quarrels, 45
and like to have fought one.

JAQ. And how was that ta'en up?

TOUCH. Faith, we met, and found the quarrel was upon the
seventh cause.

JAQ. How seventh cause? Good my lord, like this fellow. 50

DUKE S. I like him very well.

TOUCH. God 'ild you, sir; I desire you of the like. I press in
here, sir, amongst the rest of the country copulatives, to
swear and to forswear, according as marriage binds and
blood breaks. A poor virgin, sir, an ill-favour'd thing, 55
sir, but mine own. A poor humour of mine, sir, to take
that that no man else will. Rich honesty dwells like a
miser, sir, in a poor house, as your pearl in your foul
oyster.

DUKE S. By my faith, he is very swift and sententious. 60

TOUCH. According to the fool's bolt, sir, and such dulcet
diseases.

52 *God 'ild you* God yield (reward) you. *I desire you of the like* I wish the
same to you. A polite phrase in replying to good wishes or compliments. Touchstone uses it comically, as if he had said: "I hope I shall like you as well as you
like me." There is also a slight pun on "like" [K]. 53 *the country copulatives*
the rustics who wish to be coupled; the candidates for wedlock [K]. 55 *blood*
natural passion. *ill-favour'd* ugly. 56 *humour* whim, caprice. 57 *honesty*
chastity. 60 *swift and sententious* quick-witted and full of wise sayings. 61 *the
fool's bolt* Touchstone alludes to the Duke's word "swift." The old proverb runs,
"A fool's bolt is soon shot," i.e. fools shoot without taking aim or caring what
they are firing at — they speak before they think [K]. 61-2 *such dulcet diseases*
such pleasant ailments. To talk at random, or to speak before one thinks, may
be well called "a fool's disease." It is "dulcet" when it gives pleasure of amusement
to the hearer, as in the present case [K].

JAQ.   But, for the seventh cause. How did you find the
        quarrel on the seventh cause?

TOUCH. Upon a lie seven times removed (bear your body more   65
        seeming, Audrey): as thus, sir. I did dislike the cut of
        a certain courtier's beard. He sent me word, if I said his
        beard was not cut well, he was in the mind it was. This
        is call'd the Retort Courteous. If I sent him word again
        it was not well cut, he would send me word he cut it to   70
        please himself. This is call'd the Quip Modest. If again,
        it was not well cut, he disabled my judgment. This is
        call'd the Reply Churlish. If again, it was not well cut,
        he would answer I spake not true. This is call'd the
        Reproof Valiant. If again, it was not well cut, he would   75
        say I lie. This is call'd the Countercheck Quarrelsome;
        and so to the Lie Circumstantial and the Lie Direct.

JAQ.   And how oft did you say his beard was not well cut?

TOUCH. I durst go no further than the Lie Circumstantial, nor
        he durst not give me the Lie Direct; and so we measur'd   80
        swords and parted.

JAQ.   Can you nominate in order now the degrees of the lie?

TOUCH. O sir, we quarrel in print, by the book, as you have
        books for good manners. I will name you the degrees.
        The first, the Retort Courteous; the second, the Quip   85
        Modest; the third, the Reply Churlish; the fourth, the
        Reproof Valiant; the fifth, the Countercheck Quarrel-
        some; the sixth, the Lie with Circumstance; the seventh,
        the Lie Direct. All these you may avoid but the Lie

---

65 *seven times removed* in the seventh degree. Touchstone in what follows ridicules
the code of the "duello," the elaborate rules of behaviour which governed the
fighting of duels and the preservation of gentlemanly honour.   66 *seeming*
seemly.   72 *disabled* disqualified, denigrated.   76 *Countercheck* contradiction.
77 *Circumstantial* indirect.   84 *books for good manners* Courtesy books were very
popular in Shakespeare's day.   91 *take up* settle.   98 *stalking horse* any portable
object (whether the figure of a horse or not) under cover of which the hunter
can "stalk" his intended prize, i.e. get within shooting distance unseen [K].
98-9 *under the presentation of that* under the cover of his folly, which he holds
out before him (as a concealment) [K].   99 s.d. *Hymen* the god of marriage, a
common figure in wedding masques. As Johnson suggested, "Rosalind is imagined
by the rest of the company to be brought in by enchantment, and is therefore

Direct, and you may avoid that too, with an If. I knew   90
when seven justices could not take up a quarrel, but
when the parties were met themselves, one of them
thought but of an If: as, "If you said so, then I said
so"; and they shook hands and swore brothers. Your If
is the only peacemaker. Much virtue in If.   95

JAQ.   Is not this a rare fellow, my lord? He's as good at any-
          thing, and yet a fool.

DUKE S.   He uses his folly like a stalking horse, and under the
          presentation of that he shoots his wit.

          Enter Hymen, Rosalind, *and* Celia.
          Still music.

HYM.   Then is there mirth in heaven   100
          When earthly things made even
              Atone together.
          Good Duke, receive thy daughter;
          Hymen from heaven brought her,
              Yea, brought her hether,   105
          That thou mightst join her hand with his
          Whose heart within his bosom is.

ROS.   To you I give myself, for I am yours.   [*To* Duke.]
          To you I give myself, for I am yours.   [*To* Orlando.]

DUKE S.   If there be truth in sight, you are my daughter.   110

ORL.   If there be truth in shape, you are my Rosalind.

PHE.   If sight and shape be true,
          Why then, my love adieu!

---

introduced by a supposed aerial being in the character of Hymen." The act
from line 100 to the end, is, in truth, nothing but a little masque — a fore-
runner of the splendid masque in THE TEMPEST. Masques were common at stately
weddings [K].   100 *mirth* joy — not "merriment" [K].   101 *made even* reconciled.
102 *Atone together* are brought together in harmony; literally, are set "at one"
[K].   105 *hether* hither (a common Elizabethan form, preserved for the sake of
the rhyme).   106 *her hand* F³; F¹: "his hand."   107 *his bosom* F¹; some editors
would read "her bosom." But the antecedent of "Whose" is "her" in line 106.
The Duke is to join Rosalind's hand to Orlando's; her heart is already in
Orlando's bosom [K].   110 *If there be truth in sight* if my eyes do not deceive
me [K].

ROS. I'll have no father, if you be not he.   [*To* Duke.]
      I'll have no husband, if you be not he.   [*To* Orlando.] 115
      Nor ne'er wed woman, if you be not she.   [*To* Phebe.]

HYM.   Peace ho! I bar confusion.
          'Tis I must make conclusion
              Of these most strange events.
          Here's eight that must take hands   120
          To join in Hymen's bands,
              If truth holds true contents.
          You and you no cross shall part.
                        [*To* Orlando *and* Rosalind.]
          You and you are heart in heart.
                        [*To* Oliver *and* Celia.]
          You to his love must accord,   [*To* Phebe.] 125
          Or have a woman to your lord.
          You and you are sure together
                        [*To* Touchstone *and* Audrey.]
          As the winter to foul weather.
          Whiles a wedlock hymn we sing,
          Feed yourselves with questioning,   130
          That reason wonder may diminish
          How thus we met, and these things finish.

                        Song.

          Wedding is great Juno's crown —
              O blessed bond of board and bed!
          'Tis Hymen peoples every town;   135
              High wedlock then be honoured.

122 *If truth . . . true contents* "if there be truth in truth" (Johnson). Hymen's
verses are not more powerful than those of the general run of allegorical characters in masques, but there is no reason to regard them as un-Shakespearean. They
are quite good enough for the purpose [K].   123 *cross* disagreement.   125 *accord*
agree.   126 *to* for.   127 *sure together* joined in firm union.   131 *That reason
wonder may diminish* that a reasonable explanation may diminish your amaze-
ment [K].   132 *finish* come to a fit end.   133 *crown* crowning glory — for Juno
is the goddess of marriage [K].   136 *High* Probably an adverb modifying "honoured," as the next line suggests; perhaps an adjective with "wedlock," for
"wedding is great Juno's crown" [K].   140 *in no less degree* She is welcome in

Honour, high honour, and renown
To Hymen, god of every town!

DUKE S.   O my dear niece, welcome thou art to me,
Even daughter, welcome, in no less degree!   140

PHE.   [*to* Silvius] I will not eat my word, now thou art mine;
Thy faith my fancy to thee doth combine.

Enter Second Brother, [Jaques de Boys].

2. BRO.   Let me have audience for a word or two.
I am the second son of old Sir Rowland
That bring these tidings to this fair assembly.   145
Duke Frederick, hearing how that every day
Men of great worth resorted to this forest,
Address'd a mighty power, which were on foot
In his own conduct, purposely to take
His brother here and put him to the sword;   150
And to the skirts of this wild wood he came,
Where, meeting with an old religious man,
After some question with him, was converted
Both from his enterprise and from the world,
His crown bequeathing to his banish'd brother,   155
And all their lands restor'd to them again
That were with him exil'd. This to be true
I do engage my life.

DUKE S.   Welcome, young man.
Thou offer'st fairly to thy brothers' wedding:
To one, his lands withheld; and to the other,   160
A land itself at large, a potent dukedom.
First, in this forest let us do those ends

the degree that his own daughter would be welcome, rather than in that lower
degree of a mere niece.   141 *eat my word* break my promise.   142 *fancy* love.
147 *great worth* noble rank.   148 *Address'd . . . power* prepared a mighty
force.   149 *In his own conduct* under his own command.   *take* capture.   152
religious man member of a religious order; a hermit, doubtless [K].   153 *question*
conference.   156 *them* ROWE; F¹: "him."   158 *engage* pledge.   159 *Thou offer'st
. . . wedding* you make fine wedding presents at your brothers' marriage [K].
160 *one* Oliver, whose lands had been seized by Duke Frederick (III.I) [K].   *the
other* Orlando, who will succeed to the dukedom in the right of his wife, Rosalind
[K].   161 *at large* in full possession.   162 *do those ends* complete those purposes.

That here were well begun and well begot;
And after, every of this happy number
That have endur'd shrewd days and nights with us   165
Shall share the good of our returned fortune,
According to the measure of their states.
Meantime forget this new-fall'n dignity
And fall into our rustic revelry.
Play, music, and you brides and bridegrooms all,   170
With measure heap'd in joy, to th' measures fall.

JAQ.   Sir, by your patience. If I heard you rightly,
The Duke hath put on a religious life
And thrown into neglect the pompous court.

2. BRO. He hath.   175

JAQ.   To him will I. Out of these convertites
There is much matter to be heard and learn'd.
[*To* Duke] You to your former honour I bequeath;
Your patience and your virtue well deserves it.
[*To* Orlando] You to a love that your true faith doth
        merit;   180
[*To* Oliver] You to your land and love and great allies;
[*To* Silvius] You to a long and well-deserved bed;
[*To* Touchstone] And you to wrangling, for thy loving
        voyage
Is but for two months victuall'd. — So, to your pleasures!
I am for other than for dancing measures.   185

DUKE S. Stay, Jaques, stay.

JAQ.   To see no pastime I! What you would have
I'll stay to know at your abandon'd cave.   *Exit.*

---

163 *begot* conceived.   164 *every* every one.   165 *shrewd* sharp, bitter.   167 *states* ranks, conditions in life.   171 *measures* dancing. Masques regularly ended with a dance [K].   172 *by your patience* with your permission.   174 *pompous* magnificent — not in the derogatory sense [K].   176 *convertites* religious converts.   178 *bequeath* Jaques's valedictory is significantly put into the form of a last will and testament. As Furness remarks, Jaques was to join the repentant Duke in his religious life, becoming dead to the world [K].   184 *victuall'd* provided with food. 188 *stay to know* await to learn.

EPILOGUE. 2 *unhandsome* unbecoming.   3 *good wine needs no bush* One of the

DUKE S. Proceed, proceed. We will begin these rites,
　　　　As we do trust they'll end, in true delights.　[*A dance.*] 190

[EPILOGUE.]

ROS.　It is not the fashion to see the lady the epilogue; but
it is no more unhandsome than to see the lord the pro-
logue. If it be true that good wine needs no bush, 'tis
true that a good play needs no epilogue. Yet to good
wine they do use good bushes, and good plays prove the　5
better by the help of good epilogues. What a case am I
in then, that am neither a good epilogue, nor cannot
insinuate with you in the behalf of a good play! I am
not furnish'd like a beggar; therefore to beg will not
become me. My way is to conjure you, and I'll begin　10
with the women. I charge you, O women, for the love
you bear to men, to like as much of this play as please
you; and I charge you, O men, for the love you bear to
women (as I perceive by your simp'ring none of you
hates them), that between you and the women the play　15
may please. If I were a woman, I would kiss as many of
you as had beards that pleas'd me, complexions that lik'd
me, and breaths that I defied not; and I am sure, as many
as have good beards, or good faces, or sweet breaths, will,
for my kind offer, when I make curtsy, bid me farewell.　20
　　　　　　　　　　　　　　　　　　　　Exeunt.

---

best-known proverbs, though the ivy bush (sacred to Bacchus) is no longer the
vintner's sign [K].　6 *case* situation, predicament.　8 *insinuate with you* ingratiate
myself with you.　9 *furnish'd* equipped — with the usual rags and cup for alms.
10 *conjure* adjure, call upon solemnly.　15–16 *the play may please* There is a
bawdy quibble on "play."　16 *If I were a woman* Women's parts were played
by boys.　17–18 *that lik'd me* that I liked.　18 *defied* rejected (presumably because of their odour).